Low-Carb for Life

A Diet for Life
and a
Cookbook
for Success

Low-Carb for ♥ Life

A Diet for Life
and a
Cookbook for Success

by
Richard Frankville, D.C.

Unlimited Publishing
Bloomington, Indiana

Distributing Publisher:
Unlimited Publishing LLC
Bloomington, Indiana
http://www.unlimitedpublishing.com

UNLIMITED
PUBLISHING

Contributing Publisher:
Richard Frankville, D.C.
http://www.lowcarbforlife.net

Cover and book design by SSDesign, Vista, California, a work for hire, Copyright © 2004 by Unlimited Publishing LLC. This book was designed with Adobe® Lucida Bright® and Lucida Calligraphy® in Adobe® Pagemaker® software. This book makes use of one or more typefaces specifically licensed by and customized for the exclusive use of Unlimited Publishing LLC.

Unlimited Publishing LLC provides worldwide book design, printing, marketing and distribution services for professional writers and small to mid-size presses, serving as distributing publisher. Sole responsibility for the content of each work rests with the author(s) and/or contributing publisher(s). The opinions expressed herein may not be interpreted in any way as representing those of Unlimited Publishing, nor any of its affiliates.

First Edition.

Copies of this fine book and many others are available to order online at:
http://www.unlimitedpublishing.com/authors

ISBN 1-58832-097-9
Unlimited Publishing LLC
Bloomington, Indiana

Important Notices:

The ideas offered in this book are based on the author's personal experience, and experience with patients, but must not be used as a substitute for the advice and counsel of your personal physician. This is especially important if you are currently monitoring blood sugar, or taking medications such as diuretics, insulin or other diabetes medications. Consult your physician before beginning Dr. Frankville's diet program. Your physician may need to monitor your blood glucose levels more closely, as well as the dosage of your medications, due to the decreasing glucose levels that will naturally occur with this diet. Individuals with kidney disease should consult their physicians before any diet modifications. Protein levels in this diet may exceed levels that would be safe for some to follow. This diet may not be appropriate for pregnant women or nursing mothers. Consult your physician if you are pregnant or nursing before you begin this diet.

The companies and products cited in this book have been referenced solely for their excellence in quality and taste. None of these references imply that the products are intended to assist in weight loss. The companies and products cited are not in any way affiliated with the book, the author, or others involved in the book's publication. Those cited are not responsible for, nor do they endorse, the recipes or other material in this book. All companies and products cited in this book are referenced with permission.

"KNORR" is a registered trademark of Unilever Bestfoods affiliated companies, which have no connection with and do not endorse any of the recipes or other material in this book. Used with permission.

Special Thanks

Thank God for friends. I would like to offer a word of thanks to my friends who so unselfishly gave of themselves to help get this book finished.

A very special thanks to Dawn and Jeff Cope for so graciously welcoming the photo session in their home with their incredibly beautiful kitchen and an equally special thanks to their kitchen designer Patricia Redenbarger, CKD of Kitchens and Interiors, Inc. for pairing us up. Pat, you couldn't have chosen a better setting or more wonderful people to work with.

Additional thanks to Lisa Eckard, of Eckard Photography for your dedication to this project. Your photography is fabulous.

Thanks to: Wendy, for your hours of editing; Justin Boyd for your help with the spreadsheet and formatting; Stella Trotter for the hours of word processing it took to enter all of the hand written recipes and reading my chicken scratch; Dion Jones for the legal advice.

Low-Carb for Life

A Diet for Life and a Cookbook for Success
by
Richard Frankville, D.C.

Table of Contents

Acknowledgements

After many months of trial and error, I finally found a diet that changed my life forever, and gave me a new lease on... not just life, but also how I felt about myself. For this opportunity I owe a great deal of thanks and respect to my wife Sandy. There were times when I'm sure she didn't want to hear the words "fish for dinner again" let alone another word about carbohydrates. Thank you for your patience, and your help cleaning the kitchen!

My sons Alex and Austin: thank you for understanding how important this book is to me, and for giving me the peace to compose it.

I would also like to thank the rest of my family and friends, my unwavering taste testers. I spent the last two years telling my patients about this book and my recipes, and thank you for your encouragement and your patience waiting for the book.

I nearly drove the manager of my local grocery store to the edge of insanity over the last two years, keeping my kitchen well stocked. Thank you, Randy, your cooperation and assistance was priceless.

Thanks to my parents and parents-in-law for all of your support, and for always encouraging me in the pursuit of my dreams.

To Palmer College of Chiropractic: thank you for inspiring me.

Preface

This book is for anyone who truly wants to lose weight but hates diets.

The word "diet" has become a distasteful word in our vocabulary. I have been a practicing Chiropractor since 1993. I deal with health conditions every day that are complicated by weight. I have waged my own battles of the bulge. My downfall was my love for food. My family is of Italian decent. In our house, food is not just nourishment – it's a celebration of the soul.

The years of celebration finally caught up with me when I turned age 30. I spent three years of dieting off and on only to lose ten to 15 pounds at a time, which I quickly found again as soon as I stopped watching what I ate. Not only did I regain the weight I lost, but added two to three extra pounds with each successive diet failure.

Eventually I found myself buying trousers with waistline measurements larger than my age, dreadful! The real shocker was when we picked up our photos of Christmas and asked, "who's that fat man hugging our kids?" I nearly died when I realized it was me. It was at that point that I knew something had to be done! I tried the total protein diet, fat free diet, even organized weigh-in diets. All of them lacked variety, taste, and most of all, *fulfillment.*

So, ask yourself these questions. Do you find yourself taking inventory of your cabinets and refrigerator every five minutes after dinner? Are you plagued by an incessant search to satisfy a craving for something salty, something sweet … a search that never seems to end? Do you yearn for five-star quality food that will fill you up yet not make you fat? Are you sick of a diet that requires a spreadsheet to keep track of your calories, fat grams etc.? If you answer yes to one of these questions, this book is for you! Read on…

The worst things about most diet books are the long drawn-out chapters that go into minute detail about the human metabolism and simply confuse most people. As a Chiropractor, if I have learned anything about conveying ideas to patients about their bodies and their health, it is to keep the principles simple and easy to follow.

In this diet, I combined the principles of several diets and applied my own knowledge of the human metabolism. The outcome was phenomenal. I lost ten pounds within two weeks and then the rate of weight loss slowed to about one to one and a half pounds per week consistently. Collectively I shed 52 pounds in ten months.

I exercised only for the last four months of the diet, using a Torso Track machine daily for toning. I am not telling you that you don't need to exercise; in fact, alternating cardiovascular and strength training every other day will help increase your ability to burn fat. I also know that when you're heavy, it is hard to get motivated to exercise – either out of lack of energy or low sense of self-esteem. For me, it was both. So when I shed some fat, I finally had the energy to do something physical but I opted to stay home with my own equipment until I felt more secure about my appearance. Trust me: when you hit that mark where you feel good and believe that you look good too, you will be amazed at how differently the world appears. Use this book consistently and you too can share results like these.

Low-Carb for Life

A Diet for Life
and a
Cookbook for Success

About Dr. Frankville's Diet Program

The Rules

The rules are simple and the cookbook portion of this book is designed to help you stick to your guns to get skinny. I have included chapters to help get you through breakfast, lunch and dinner so use the cook book religiously. I promise you, your taste buds won't get bored if you do.

Try to eat a minimum of three times per day. If your schedule permits, I encourage you to eat five smaller meals per day. Eat a sensible light breakfast. Have a piece of fruit in the mid-morning hours if possible; at lunch time, you will be less tempted to gorge at a buffet. For lunch, choose a salad or lettuce sandwich. (We will discuss these later.) If you suffer from afternoon munchies, a piece of fruit or some low-carb granola will help. Finally, for dinner, select one entrée (protein), one vegetable and one salad from the cookbook. I truly encourage you to make sure that at dinner you get all three: protein, vegetable and salad. This way, after your kitchen is clean and closed for the night, you will be full, and you won't be tempted to go back and graze, out of boredom or habit. Now, let's move on to the rest of the limits.

Daily Limits Allowed

> **50 grams of Complex Carbohydrate per day**

Vegetables are the best way to get these. I recommend fresh vegetables when available, but when fresh produce is not available, use frozen vegetables instead. Canned vegetables often have added sugars and have been cooked, thus providing fewer nutrients. Most grocery stores today post the nutritional values for the fresh produce they sell. These value tables are usually located below the price sign. Read the label carefully in all cases. Plan ahead with each meal. Do the math. Subtract the dietary fiber content from the carbohydrate content to find the true total carbohydrate content. Pay close attention to the amount the label indicates as one serving, as it may be unrealistically small.

To illustrate:

> **1 cup lima beans = 22 gr carb -5 gr fiber = 17 grams carb**

Lima beans have 22 grams of carbohydrate and five grams of dietary fiber, per one cup serving. Thus, the total carbohydrate content is 17 grams of carbohydrate per serving.

While 17 grams may not seem like a lot, you will note as you compile your intake for the day that in the American diet carbohydrates have a tendency to add up quickly.

Pace your self for the day. Start out with a very low number of carbohydrates for breakfast, add more carbohydrates at lunch and use your remaining carbs at dinner. For example:

Breakfast

Item	Carbohydrate (grams)
Two eggs prepared any way you like them	0
Bacon, sausage, lox (smoked salmon), unlimited	0
½ grapefruit	about 10
Coffee	0
Total	**10 grams**

Lunch

Item	Carbohydrate (grams)
Grilled Chicken Caesar Salad with croutons	about 12
Iced tea	0
Total	**12 grams**

Dinner

Item	Carbohydrate (grams)
Grilled Swordfish with Ginger Lime Pesto	0
Savory Beans	about 14
One 6 ounces glass of wine	about 10
Total	**24 grams**

Total for the day: 46 grams, leaving 4 grams to spare for a snack

Protein Unlimited

Fish is the best way to go. You can eat a lot of it without the extra fat contained in other meats. It's also very easy for most people to digest. Fish is also loaded with Omega 3 fats that are powerful anti-oxidants for the body, which help prevent heart disease and certain types of cancer. Chicken is the next best protein choice, as it is also low in fat and easily digested. Pork, while delicious, can be more difficult to digest and is higher in fat content, so moderate your intake; once a week as an entrée is plenty. Beef, while high in protein, is also higher in fat than other proteins, so be conservative with its intake. If you are watching your cholesterol intake, you may want to limit your intake of beef. You will notice that I have not included recipes for beef in this book. The reason is simply because everyone knows how to prepare beef, and there are an abundance of recipes available. You will also note that if beef, chicken or pork can be substituted in the recipes contained in this book, it is stated as a footnote at the bottom of the recipe.

Lastly, if you're not familiar with the concept of eating for your blood type, I recommend you give the book, *Eat Right 4 Your Type* a glance. I have personally found some validity to many of the points made in the book about digestibility of different foods.

Fat Unlimited

Use common sense here: don't eat excessive amounts of fat and don't use non-fat substitutes, as they are usually loaded with sugars to boost the taste. I encourage the use of pure, naturally occurring fats, like butter and Olive oil, as opposed to fake fats like margarine. Use real dairy. If you wish to cut back on the fat in my recipes, you can easily substitute half-and-half for heavy cream, or whole milk for half-and-half. You can cut as much fat as you like with your choice of milk fat content, but remember that you may need to thicken the sauces. I suggest using cheeses to thicken sauces, instead of flour or cornstarch, to keep the dishes low in carbohydrate. Monterey jack, brie, gruyere and cream cheese are some of the easiest to use. Please also keep in mind that the less milk fat, the higher the sugar content, so be careful – don't add sugar to spare a little fat!

Vegetables Unlimited

Watch the bean and pea families; they usually have higher carbohydrate content than you may think. Vegetables are wonderful for many reasons: for one, they are unlimited in this diet, and there's no better way to get full and stay full than with vegetables. Gorging yourself is never recommended, but if you must gorge on anything it should be vegetables or salad. So if you're *really* hungry, reach for a bucket-o-salad or veggies. One trick to offset a few more carbohydrates is to consume high quality carbohydrates like vegetables with high fiber content, such as green beans, Lima beans, fennel, celery, lettuce, spinach, etc.

There are two kinds of dietary fiber, soluble and insoluble. Luckily most fruits and vegetables posses both soluble and insoluble dietary fiber. Insoluble fiber is the component responsible for preventing your body from absorbing some of the carbohydrate content of foods. It acts like a dietary "eraser" when it comes to carbohydrates. Insoluble fiber keeps the intestinal tract regular and may help to prevent certain types of cancer. Soluble fiber is thought to help control blood sugar and may even help prevent heart disease.

Vegetables are low in fat content, and rich in vitamins and minerals that our bodies need to thrive. They also contain powerful antioxidants, which help prevent cancer. Many vegetables also contain different types of highly absorbable calcium, which is an essential element for fighting osteoporosis and maintaining healthy bones. There are several different kinds of calcium. All of them are required in this diet, to ensure that your body is getting its daily requirements. Many people take oyster shell based calcium supplements daily, and believe that they are getting everything they need. The truth is that they are getting only one kind of calcium, which does not fulfill all of the body's needs. Eating a greater quantity and variety of fruits and vegetables daily will help fulfil your body's daily requirements. If you do supplement your calcium intake, make sure that you are taking a complete calcium supplement that is high in absorbability. Most nutrition stores and chiropractors sell complete calcium supplements.

Snacks

Snacks in this diet (at least while you are in a weight reduction mode) are discouraged. If you're a snacker, think of cavemen: in other words, anything you could hunt or forage is acceptable: fruit, nuts, berries and the like.

Nuts: ½ cup per day allowed, not required. Soy nuts are nearly pure protein and have no carbohydrates unless they are coated with a seasoned salt, which will add only trace amounts of carbohydrates to the total carb count. Walnuts are another great choice as they are virtually carb-free and contain fats that are good for you.

Fruit: Two pieces per day are recommended, but no bananas, which are high in carbohydrate content.

Cheese: 3 ounces per day allowed, not required.

For those moments when you just can't take it anymore, and there will be a few, I have found a couple of companies that I love for their low-carb products when it comes to snacking.

LowCarb Success: A company out of Hutto, Texas, makes a granola that will knock your socks off.

Specialty Cheese Company: Makes chips out of grated cheese and uses wonderful cheeses like jalepeno jack cheese and white Cheddar. For a chip substitute that you can either munch or dip, I have found none better. If you can't find these products in your grocery or health food store, look in the specialty food reference section in the back of this book and call them. You won't be sorry!

Pure De-Lite Belgian Chocolate: Makes an unbelievable chocolate that is so good you will never know it's low-carb. These lovely little morsels of pleasure only have a couple of grams of carbohydrate per serving, and make a really nice treat once in a while.

"NO-NO's"

No sugar, raw or processed: think of sugar as **POISON**; it will keep you hungry and fat. If you need sweetener, use SPLENDA™ Granular.

No sugar-laden beverages, including juice: we often don't think about the things we drink, but should. Most prepared juices bought in stores are loaded with sugar. Orange juice is a prime example. Prepared orange juice on average contains 27 grams of carbohydrate per eight fluid ounce serving. That's more than 25% of your daily allowance of carbohydrate. If you must drink juice, avoid those with added sugars. Best advice: get a juicer! Be careful with soft drinks as well. The average cola-type soft drink contains 40 grams of carbohydrate per 12-ounce serving.

Limit your alcohol intake: If you drink an alcoholic beverage, have just one per day. Try sticking with wine. Wine has the least effect on fat retention. According to a recent study, wine drinkers showed the lowest amount of body fat, especially through the middle.

No bread: it might taste good, but it keeps you fat. Bread is highly glycolic and really a waste of carbs. If you are fortunate enough to live in an area where you can find truly low-carb bread (six to eight grams or less per slice) then you can have one slice per day.

No potatoes: they are one of the most glycolic, sugar-producing foods around.

No rice: it's essentially a yummy culinary filler that is loaded with carbohydrates. The only kind of rice that is acceptable in small amounts is wild rice. It's high enough in fiber and doesn't gain extra carbs from processing.

No cereal: almost every cereal on the market today has added sugar and uses high-carb ingredients. The only cereal I have found that is acceptable is from LowCarb Success. Their granola has only two grams of effective carbohydrate per ½ cup serving. If you find any other cereal out there that can match or beat that, not only can you have it, but let me know – I want it too!

No pasta: believe it or not, this Italian is turning down his staple of heritage – so don't tell me you can't live without pasta. You may as well sing to the choir. If you insist on having pasta, my advice is to try a soy-based pasta to decrease the carbohydrate content. Or save up carbs for a week, and have a beautiful plate of the real stuff on Sunday.

No corn or corn products: due to the highly glycolic nature of this food group.

No chips or crackers: aside from the cheese chips previously mentioned. Soy chips are also available. Some folks like them. When it comes to crackers, my best advice is *read the labels!* If they are low enough in carbohydrate content to be acceptable and you are willing to sacrifice the carbs, then go ahead. Crackers are low enough in carbohydrate content if five crackers equal 14 grams of carbohydrate or less. Add some cheese, a sliced apple and a big glass of ice water; it makes a nice treat a couple of times per week.

The Science Simplified

This diet is simple. The only thing you must remember is that the human body requires 40 grams of glucose per day to maintain a healthy nervous system. In other words, feed your brain a minimum of 40 grams of glucose per day. Glucose is a dietary sugar found in carbohydrates. Carbohydrates are chains of dietary sugar molecules: glucose, galactose, ribose, lactose, maltose and fructose. Most carbohydrates contain more glucose than any other dietary sugars except fruit, which is almost purely fructose. So if your brain requires 40 grams of glucose per day and you eat foods that collectively add up to 40 grams of carbohydrate, you have just satisfied your body's daily need for glucose.

I tried to limit myself to precisely 40 grams of carbohydrate and found myself constantly hungry. Increasing my maximum daily intake to 50 grams did the trick. Finally, I was satisfied.

The reason it is so important to limit the number of carbohydrates ingested daily is because carbs break down to glucose molecules or sugar, which keeps you hungry. The sugar cycle is a hard habit to break. It will take about a week to get through the withdrawal process.

Another reason to avoid excessive carbohydrate intake is that the body can only metabolize so much glucose at a time by insulin production. The remaining unused glucose will go one of two paths. One way is through the kidneys and out of the body via the urinary tract. This is very hard on the kidneys as the glucose molecules are very large and can cause deterioration leading to kidney disease. The other more common route the excess glucose takes is called the Krebs cycle. This is where the body will convert and store the excess glucose as fat, saving it for later use – making you fatter. When you're low on glucose in the bloodstream, the body then will convert fat into ketones, which can be used like glucose; this is called ketosis. The body can tolerate a state of ketosis only for short periods of time, as it is hard on the central nervous system.

Protein in this diet is unlimited, as it is used quickly in the body. But proteins should be graded. Soy is the *best* source of protein available. Fish is an *excellent* source of protein, rich in minerals and vitamins and relatively low in fat. Chicken is a *good* source of protein, provided that the skin and fat are removed. Pork and beef are *fair* sources of protein; the fat content and digestibility actually reduce their value as a protein source.

I agree with the theory that it takes fat to burn fat as suggested in almost all of the high protein diet books, such as the one by the late Dr. Atkins. I prefer to get those fats naturally from sources that are actually fatty rather than proteins laden with fat. You will note in the recipes in this book that much of the fat in this diet comes from dairy and olive oil. A note here of extreme importance: for years people have been poisoning themselves with margarine. The human body produces fat cutting/dissolving enzymes called lipase, literally meaning "to break down fats." The human body has never produced an enzyme to break down fake fats like margarine, and consequently we have seen a rise in cardiovascular disease. Margarine basically turns into a sticky sludge on the arterial walls, and later tuns into a plaque-like substance that can't be removed non-invasively. So do yourself a favor: throw out fake fats now, and thank me when you're 90!

The Importance of Water

Most of the time when people think they are hungry, they're actually thirsty... that's right, thirsty! Most people are in a state of mild dehydration much of the time. I know we drink a lot of beverages, but there's not a soda, coffee, tea or juice that even comes close to the power to re-hydrate the body of water. Simply stated: *most people don't drink nearly enough water.* Ideally, we should take in one gallon of water per day, and spaced over the course of the entire day. If you consume a whole gallon of water in the evening hours when at rest, not only will you not get much rest that night, but your body won't absorb as much as you need. The body can only process so much water at a time, like a storm drain; too much volume and the excess just runs over.

Philosophy and Strategy

Mindset is of vital importance. The way I kept my eating in check was by changing the way I looked at what I was eating. I wasn't losing weight; I was getting thin. Loss has negative connotations. Remember to remain positive whenever speaking about your efforts. Approach anything on the "No-No" list as **POISON**. Stay off the scales. Weigh in before beginning your program and not again for another week. Weighing too often will not show you a realistic rate of achievement and may discourage you. Inevitably you will go out for lunch or dinner. Friends will invite you to dinner. You will be invited to a party where snacks will be present. With all of these pitfalls, your mindset can save your waistline!

When lunching out, always look at the salad section of the menu. Most restaurants have a salad menu that includes a grilled chicken breast or a piece of grilled fish. Look carefully at the description of the salad. If they list croutons, potatoes or corn, you can ask the waiter to have those ingredients removed.

When invited by friends to dinner, forget about the traditional gift of wine. Offer to bring a salad to complement the meal, and sneak in a fresh fruit compote for desert. When your hosts say "You shouldn't have," simply reply that you had the fruit in the 'fridge and it was so dead ripe that it would have spoiled if it went another day uneaten!

When invited to a party, always ask if you can bring a relish tray. If they ask you to bring chips instead, tell the hosts that you have fresh veggies and won't have the opportunity to use them, so you would really like to bring those too. Most people will graciously accept. If you follow these simple strategies for social gatherings, you will always have something that you can eat!

How to Use the Cookbook

My patients and I have a great rapport, and most of them know that my favorite hobby is gourmet cooking. Over the years, I have been asked many times for recipes. Once in a while, someone would relate to me that they had modified the recipe by adding this or exchanging that. This used to really get me steamed. After all, in my opinion those recipes were perfected by me and didn't need any help. But then I noticed that I too was guilty of the same crime. I realized then what a great idea it would be to make a cookbook with my recipes on one side of the book, and a facing page for your own notes, as you will see inside.

I wish you much success with your efforts, and welcome any feedback about the program and the recipes. If you have questions about the recipes or diet, feel free to call or write. I love getting letters about my patients' successes too. I would enjoy hearing from you. Best wishes and best of luck!

Buon Appetito,

Dr. Richard Frankville

Breakfast

Breakfast

Unfortunately we have all been raised with visions of pancakes, waffles, biscuits and gravy, or toast and jelly whenever someone mentions breakfast. The one thing they all have in common is that they are loaded with carbohydrates. At some point in our past, someone decided that we needed to load up on calories in the morning to have enough "energy" for the day. Although traditional breakfast foods taste great, this philosophy actually gives us an extra load of fat to burn off before we can get to work on the reserve fat we are carrying around on our tushies!.

Luckily, due to the growing interest in low-carb dieting, there is an abundance of products available now for those of us who would rather live low carb, allowing us to remain puritanical in our pursuit. That's right: we are no longer limited to eggs, fruit, ricotta or cottage cheese, or yogurt for breakfast. And, thanks to these wonderful products, we no longer fall victim to ridiculous recipes that require us to seek out ingredients on our own like whey protein powder, guar gum and psyllium husks used to make bread products or pancakes.

The best thing is many items are now available in quick mixes that are practical for daily use – and they taste great! The company **LowCarb Success** has successfully put pancakes, muffins, waffles, granola and even hot cereals back on our menu. This company has created incredibly delicious low-carb pancakes and waffles in flavors like Butter Pecan, Banana Walnut and Apple Spice. The coolest thing (aside from the fact that they taste great) is that they contain only two grams of effective carbohydrate per pancake or waffle... wow! The hot cereals, equally incredible, come in Vanilla Almond, Butter Pecan, Apple Spice and Strawberries and Cream. Carb count on these range from only one to two grams of effective carbohydrate per serving. I'm not kidding: for those of you who have tried the other low-carb diets and simply become sick of eating meat and cheese, these products will add a whole new dimension to your world! If your grocery store doesn't carry their products, please take a moment to speak with the store manager. With the growing demand for products that are low in carbohydrate, they will consider adding these items to their shelves, or, at minimum, offer to special order them for you.

The next topic for breakfast is eggs. They are safe to eat more frequently than we have been told in the past. As researchers have had the opportunity to gather information over the last few years, they are finally changing their tune on cholesterol levels relative to egg consumption. For the skeptics, however, it is OK to use egg substitutes instead. Omelets are a nice way to get more variety in your breakfast menu, but require some prep time. "Prep time?" I can hear you asking. I know first hand that most people today are rushed and time is of the essence in every aspect of our lives. We get up with only moments to spare, thanks to the advent of the snooze button. We rush our families through a quickie breakfast, barking at them to get dressed and ready for school or work, all the while reminding them and ourselves that we're going to be late if we don't get going. And I have the audacity to expect you to follow this diet at breakfast? Well, YES!

To help make all of this easier, you need a few things to help organize your process. First get a divided plastic or rubber container like the ones used to store a relish tray. Get a hand food chopper. You can find these at any decent kitchen gadget shop. Buy a microwave omelet maker or simply use an old margarine container; they work great. Next designate one hour or so on the weekend to slice, dice, and chop up all of your favorite vegetables, meats and cheeses for omelets. As far as meats go, you can fry and crumble bacon and sausage both, which keep very well in the fridge. Use deli meats too; julienne slice ham and turkey cold cuts and buy your favorite cheeses pre-shredded to help keep your mornings simple. To save yourself time make the omelet in the microwave. This not only saves time, but it cuts down on dishes. Oh, and about dishes, dieting is tough enough, so give yourself permission to leave a few dishes in the sink in the morning. You can take care of them when you get home.

Omelet Instructions for the Microwave

For a single serving omelet beat two eggs with one tablespoon of heavy whipping cream. Pour the egg mixture into the microwave omelet dish or old margarine container and add your favorite ingredients, one teaspoon of each, to the egg mixture. If you are using an Egg Substitute use ½ cup per person. Microwave on high for 35 seconds for a loose omelet, or one minute for an omelet that is cooked through. Here are some pan-cooked omelets to give you some ideas to get started. Let your imagination run wild. Omelets are one of the most subjective and versatile meals you can make.

Bacon and Cauliflower Omelet

Serves 1 to 2

4 eggs beaten well

1 tablespoon heavy whipping cream

½ cup bacon cut into ½ inch strips and fried crisp

¼ cup cauliflower chopped

2 scallions chopped fine

¼ cup Swiss cheese grated

2 tablespoons butter

To Prepare:

In a mixing bowl, combine the eggs and cream and beat together well. In a non-stick skillet over medium heat, melt the butter. Add the beaten eggs and cream. Using a wooden spoon, stir the bottom of the skillet gently. Essentially, you're trying to make a solid wet pancake of egg. Push the uncooked runny egg into any void spots or thin spots, trying to get the wet pancake even in thickness. Next add the bacon, chopped cauliflower, scallions, and Swiss cheese, sprinkling them over the entire surface of the cooking omelet. Fold the omelet in half, so all the ingredients are covered. Turn the heat to low and place sliced Swiss cheese over the top of the omelet. Cover the pan with a lid and let the cheese melt. When the cheese has melted, the omelet should be cooked through.

Broccoli, Ham and Cheese Omelet

Serves 1 to 2

4 eggs beaten well

1 tablespoon heavy whipping cream

¼ cup broccoli florets chopped

¼ cup ham cubed

¼ cup Cheddar cheese grated

2 tablespoons butter

To Prepare:

In a mixing bowl, combine the eggs and cream and beat together well. In a non-stick skillet over medium heat, melt the butter. Add the beaten eggs and cream. Using a wooden spoon, stir the bottom of the skillet gently. Essentially, you're trying to make a solid wet pancake of egg. Push the uncooked runny egg into any void spots or thin spots, trying to get the wet pancake even in thickness. Next add the broccoli, ham and Cheddar cheese, sprinkling them over the entire surface of the cooking omelet. Fold the omelet in half so all the ingredients are covered. Turn the heat to low, and place sliced Cheddar cheese over the top of the omelet. Cover the pan with a lid and let the cheese melt. When the cheese has melted the omelet should be cooked through.

Chef's Notes

Denver Omelet

Serves 1 to 2

4 eggs beaten well

1 tablespoon heavy whipping cream

2 scallions chopped fine

½ cup cubed ham

¼ cup green or red pepper diced

¼ cup marble Cheddar cheese grated

2 tablespoons butter

To Prepare:

In a mixing bowl, combine the eggs and cream and beat together well. In a non-stick skillet over medium heat, melt the butter. Add the beaten eggs and cream. Using a wooden, spoon stir the bottom of the skillet gently. Essentially you're trying to make a solid wet pancake of egg. Push the uncooked runny egg into any void spots or thin spots trying to get the wet pancake even in thickness. Next add the ham, diced pepper, and cheese sprinkling them over the entire surface of the cooking omelet. Fold the omelet in half, so all the ingredients are covered. Turn the heat to low and place sliced marble Cheddar over the top of the omelet. Cover the pan with a lid and let the cheese melt. When the cheese has melted, the omelet should be cooked through. This makes a great meal for one if you're starving, or a light meal for two.

Chef's Notes

Mediterranean Tomato Omelet

Serves 1 to 2

4 eggs beaten well

1 tablespoon heavy whipping cream

1/2 cup Italian plumb tomatoes, de-seeded and diced

1/4 cup feta cheese

2 scallions chopped fine

1 clove garlic, minced

1 tablespoon fresh basil leaves chopped

2 tablespoons butter

To Prepare:

In a mixing bowl, combine the eggs and cream and beat together well. In a non-stick skillet over medium heat, melt the butter. Add the beaten eggs and cream. Using a wooden spoon, stir the bottom of the skillet gently. Essentially, you're trying to make a solid wet pancake of egg. Push the uncooked runny egg into any void spots or thin spots, trying to get the wet pancake even in thickness. Next add the tomatoes, feta cheese, chopped scallions, garlic and basil. Sprinkle the ingredients over the entire surface of the cooking omelet. Fold the omelet in half so all the ingredients are covered. Turn the heat to low. Cover the pan with a lid and let the omelet cook for about four minutes.

Mushroom and Cheese Omelet

Serves 1 to 2

4 eggs beaten well

1 tablespoon heavy whipping cream

1/3 cup fresh mushrooms, chopped

2 scallions chopped fine

1/4 cup Swiss cheese, grated

2 tablespoons butter

To Prepare:

In a mixing bowl, combine the eggs and cream and beat together well. In a non-stick skillet over medium heat, melt the butter. Add the beaten eggs and cream. Using a wooden spoon, stir the bottom of the skillet gently. Essentially, you're trying to make a solid wet pancake of egg. Push any uncooked runny egg into void spots or thin spots, trying to get the wet pancake even in thickness. Next add the mushrooms, chopped scallions, and Swiss cheese, sprinkling them over the entire surface of the cooking omelet. Fold the omelet in half so all the ingredients are covered. Turn the heat to low, and place sliced Swiss cheese over the top of the omelet. Cover the pan with a lid and let the cheese melt. When the cheese has melted, the omelet should be done.

Chef's Notes

Salsicce and Pepperoni Omelet
Italian Sausage and Red Pepper Omelet

Serves 1 to 2

4 eggs beaten well

1 tablespoon heavy whipping cream

½ cup Italian sausage, membrane removed, fried and crumbled

¼ cup red pepper diced

⅓ cup mozzarella cheese grated

2 tablespoons butter

To Prepare:

In a mixing bowl, combine the eggs and cream and beat together well. In a non-stick skillet over medium heat, melt the butter. Add the beaten eggs and cream. Using a wooden spoon, stir the bottom of the skillet gently. Essentially, you're trying to make a solid wet pancake of egg. Push the uncooked runny egg into any void spots or thin spots, trying to get the wet pancake even in thickness. Next add the Sausage, diced pepper and cheese, sprinkling them over the entire surface of the cooking omelet. Fold the omelet in half so all the ingredients are covered. Turn the heat to low, and place sliced mozzarella cheese over the top of the omelet. Cover the pan with a lid, and let the cheese melt. When the cheese has melted, the omelet should be cooked through.

Sunny Side Up Parmesan Eggs

Serves 1

Fried eggs are an old favorite, but seem to require toast to feel complete. With my Parmesan eggs, you don't miss the toast; the whites get nice and crispy, and taste great.

2 jumbo eggs

1 tablespoon butter

2 tablespoons Parmesan cheese pre-grated, canned

¼ cup white zinfandel wine

Fresh crushed black pepper to taste

To Prepare:

In a non-stick skillet with a lid, heat the butter over medium-high heat. When the butter has melted, add the eggs to the skillet and let them fry until the white is set. Sprinkle the Parmesan cheese over the top of the eggs. Pour the white zinfandel wine around the outer edges of the eggs, cover with the lid, and let steam for about one minute. When done, the yolk should still be runny but the whites will be crispy. Serve as is; the Parmesan cheese takes away the need for toast. It's amazing: you'll never miss the bread!

Chef's Notes

_____

_____

_____

_____

_____

_____

_____

_____

_____

_____

_____

_____

Tips for Pancakes

The syrups available in the low-carb and no sugar categories that I have tried did not impress me. Instead of putting up with less than adequate tasting syrup, I butter my pancakes, then spread Estee Brand Raspberry Preserves over them instead of syrup. Between the pancakes, I spread a heaping soup spoon full of cottage cheese or ricotta. It reminds me of a blintz. Yum!

Another trick is to take ½ cup of Estee brand preserves, add ¼ cup water and one tablespoon of lemon juice, mix well, and heat in the microwave or in a saucepan over low heat. This makes a really nice fruit syrup that tastes great. Use this syrup on pancakes or waffles. For really fancy waffles, when you feel the need to feed your eyes, try whipping one cup of heavy whipping cream with two tablespoons of SPLENDA™ Granular and ½ teaspoon of vanilla. Top the waffles with the fruit syrup and dollop a big spoon of the whipped cream on top. You'll feel like you're cheating, but you're not!

Tips for Hot Cereal

The hot cereals from LowCarb Success mentioned earlier are good when prepared according to the instructions on the packages. They are even better if you use ¼ cup of heavy whipping cream or Half & Half, and ½ cup of water instead. Finally, sprinkle a tablespoon of SPLENDA™ Granular over the top, and add some butter. Wow! You can even add some fresh fruit. Try adding fresh peaches or nectarines to the Vanilla Almond flavor, and chopped apples or pears to the Cinnamon Spice flavor.

Appetizers, Soups & Salads

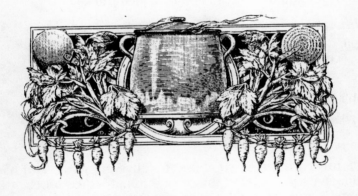

Mozzarella Insalata

Serves 4-6

There are two versions of the wonderful summer delight called Mozzarella Insalata. One version hails from the region of Modena. Since the Amalfi coast is so well known for its sun-ripened tomatoes, this version uses fresh sliced tomatoes. The other version, which is served elsewhere in Italy, uses roasted red bell peppers. The method is the essentially the same for both.

Start with a pound of fresh mozzarella cheese, removed from the brine, washed and sliced into ¼ inch thick slices. Please note that the cheese may continue to weep after it has been sliced; you may want to place the cheese in a strainer and over a bowl, and allow it to drain over night in the refrigerator.

Alla Modena

½ cup extra virgin olive oil, the darker or greener in
    color the better

1 clove garlic, minced

8-10 basil leaves sliced into thin ribbons

2 large ripe tomatoes sliced about ¼ inch thick

Traditional

½ cup extra virgin olive oil, the darker or greener in
    color the better

1 clove garlic, minced

8-10 basil leaves sliced into thin ribbons

1 jar roasted red bell peppers drained, Frieda's brand

To Prepare:

In a measuring cup, combine the olive oil, garlic and basil. For the Modena style version, place one tomato slice on each slice of mozzarella and drizzle the olive oil mixture over the tomatoes and cheese like a dressing, then serve. For the traditional style, place one pepper strip on top of each slice of mozzarella drizzle with the olive oil mixture and serve.

Chef's Notes

Red and Yellow Oven Roasted Peppers Stuffed with Crab, Lobster and Shrimp

Serves 2

4 red and 4 yellow bell peppers or 12 miniature red and yellow
  bell peppers available from most gourmet grocers

6 ounces lump crab meat, canned

6 ounces lobster slipper meat, cooked and shredded
  (or use monkfish, see below)

12 jumbo cocktail shrimp, tails removed and chopped
  medium fine

1 large clove of garlic, minced

1 shallot minced

4 ounces mascarpone cheese

2 tablespoons Parmesan cheese, in this case,
  pre-grated canned is fine

1/8 teaspoon ground white pepper

To Prepare:

Shred the lobster slipper meat into small pieces and combine in a
small mixing bowl with the crabmeat, chopped shrimp, garlic, shallot, softened mascarpone, Parmesan and white pepper. Mix until
well combined. Slice the miniature peppers in half lengthwise and
remove the seeds. If using large peppers, cut them into sections
where the fruit indents at its natural seam. Using the stuffing prepared above, fill the pepper sections to the top, but do not over-fill,
as the filling will cook over. Coat a baking dish with one or two
tablespoons of olive oil, place the stuffed peppers in the dish stuffed
side up, and bake in a 350 degree oven until lightly golden on top,
about 25 to 30 minutes. Let the peppers cool for about five minutes
before serving. These are fantastic with a salad, as an entrée, or
alone as hors d'oeuvres.

*Monkfish may be substituted for lobster, by boiling it in water
with a tablespoon of crab boil; it tastes much like lobster.*

Chef's Notes

Rumake

Serves 4-6

1 pound chicken livers, washed and excess fat removed

½ pound lean thick sliced bacon cut in half

1-6 ounce can of water chestnuts

⅓ cup soy sauce

Tooth picks to secure the Rumake

2 dashes tobasco sauce, optional

To Prepare:

Place one chicken liver and a water chestnut together, and wrap them into a tight bundle with ½ of a slice of bacon. Secure the bundle using a pair of toothpicks crosswise like an X. Place the Rumake on a baking sheet with sides to prevent runoff of any drippings in the oven. Pour the soy sauce over the Rumake and bake in a pre-heated 375-degree oven for 45 minutes to one hour, or until the Rumake are browned and the bacon is lightly crisped.

Tobasco sauce may be added to the soy sauce for some extra zing. Another interesting variation is to add a tablespoon of honey mustard and two dashes of tobasco to the soy sauce.

Delicious!

Salmon Roulades on Cucumber Chips

Serves 4-6

1 medium cucumber peeled every ⅛ of an inch, so it has a striped appearance then sliced into chips about ⅛ of an inch thick. You can rib slice the cucumber for even more decoration. Be sure to use a cucumber that isn't too seedy.

Brine:

1 cup rice wine vinegar

¼ cup water

1 tablespoon kosher salt

1 tablespoon dill

Topping:

½ pound un-salted lox, or cold smoked salmon

4 ounces cream cheese, softened

½ cup sour cream

1 teaspoon fresh chives chopped fine

1 teaspoon fresh dill chopped fine

1 teaspoon lemon juice

To Prepare:

Peel and slice the cucumber as explained above, and place the chips in a sealable plastic bag. Add rice wine vinegar, water, kosher salt and chopped dill to the bag. Close the bag and refrigerate over night to make a crisp, fresh pickle-like chip. Separate the slices of lox on a piece of waxed paper and set aside. In a small mixing bowl, combine the sour cream, softened cream cheese, chopped chives, chopped dill and lemon juice stir well. Using a rubber spatula, butter the lox slices with the sour cream mixture, as if frosting a cake. Place the dressed lox slices in the refrigerator for about one hour, so the sour cream mixture is firm. Next, remove the dressed lox from the refrigerator, and gently curl the lox into a roll, beginning at the widest end. Return the rolls to the refrigerator for another hour to firm again, or, if pressed for time, you may freeze the rolls for 15-20 minutes. While the salmon rolls are firming, empty the bag of cucumber chips into a strainer and let them drain off. Once the rolls have firmed, use a very sharp knife to slice the rolls into pinwheels about $\frac{1}{8}$ of an inch thick. Place a pinwheel slice on top of each cucumber chip, arrange on a serving tray and serve. You may prepare these earlier in the day and refrigerate until ready to serve as well.

Place a pinwheel slice on top of each cucumber chip, arrange on a serving tray and serve. You may prepare these earlier in the day and refrigerate until ready to serve as well.

Chef's Notes

Sicilian Olive Salad

Serves 20 as a relish

1 cup ripe black olives chopped

1 cup large pimento stuffed green olives, chopped

1 cup fresh or canned mushrooms, chopped

¾ cup celery, split the ribs into thirds and slice thin

1 clove garlic, minced

4 tablespoons olive oil

½ teaspoon basil flakes

½ teaspoon oregano flakes

To Prepare:

Combine all of the ingredients in a small mixing bowl and toss well. Chill over night to peak the flavor. This salad is easy, and makes a nice side dish for summer picnics or any occasion. It is used as a kind of relish served with meats or fresh sliced cheese in antipasto. My mother gets credit for this recipe, which she often served on holidays. It was the first thing everyone missed if she didn't make it.

Succulent Deviled Shrimp Stuffed Mushrooms

Serves 4 to 6

1 tablespoon butter

1 cup shrimp, shelled, cleaned, de-veined, cooked and chopped coarsely

2 scallions, whites chopped fine, greens sliced into very thin ringlets

1 clove garlic, minced

2-3 dashes cayenne pepper

1 heaping tablespoon sour cream

½ cup shredded Monterey jack cheese

½ cube KNORR® shrimp bouillon

1 shot dry vermouth

1 pound large mushrooms; cremini or moonbella are ideal

To Prepare:

Using a soft cloth, wipe off the mushroom caps to remove any debris. Gently remove the stems from the caps, cut off the woody end, and reserve the tender stem. Using a small spoon (a grapefruit spoon is ideal) gently scrape out the gills from the caps. Set aside the cleaned mushroom caps and prepare the filling.

In a non-stick skillet over medium-high heat, melt one tablespoon of butter. Add the shrimp, one shot dry vermouth and shrimp bouillon. Cook until bright pink, about three minutes. Remove from heat and transfer to a small bowl. When cool, add the sour cream, scallions, garlic and Monterey jack cheese. Gently mix, blending the ingredients well.

Stuff the mushroom caps with this mixture. Place the stuffed caps on a baking sheet and bake in a pre-heated 375-degree oven for 25 to30 minutes or until the tops are lightly golden. Serve hot. For the real heat-seekers try nixing the cayenne pepper and substitute habanero jack cheese... wow!

Chef's Notes

Summery Seafood Salad

Serves 4 to 6

1 pound frozen cocktail shrimp, defrosted, tails removed and chopped into coarse chunks

6 ounces (or 1 can) lump crab meat, drained if canned

1 container, 8 ounces, plain yogurt

2 scallions, whites finely diced and greens sliced into thin ringlets

1 tablespoon fresh dill, finely chopped

1 rib of celery, split into thirds and sliced thinly

½ lemon, juiced

¼ teaspoon curry powder

To Prepare:

In a small mixing bowl, combine all of the ingredients and toss well. Place the salad in the refrigerator to chill for at least four hours to allow the flavors to meld. Toss the salad again before serving.

Zucchini Pizza

Serves 2 to 4

4 cups coarsely grated zucchini

¼ cup olive oil

3 cloves garlic, minced

3 tablespoons oregano flakes

1 tablespoon basil flakes

1 teaspoon "reduced" salt: *salt with low sodium content*

2 cups shredded mozzarella cheese

½ cup grated Parmesan cheese; canned is best in this case

To Prepare:

Heat the olive oil in a non-stick skillet over medium-high heat, add the grated zucchini, garlic, oregano, basil, and salt. Sauté until tender, about 8-10 minutes. Remove from heat and set aside. Line a sided baking sheet with aluminum foil and pre-heat your oven to 350-degrees. Spoon the zucchini mixture out onto the foil and use a rubber spatula to spread the mixture into a rectangle shape about ³/₄ of an inch thick. Sprinkle the Parmesan cheese over the top, then repeat this step using the mozzarella cheese. Place the assembled pizza into the oven and bake for about 25-30 minutes or until the cheese on top is bubbly and lightly golden. Remove from the oven and let it cool for about ten minutes to set, then cut the pizza into squares and serve. Please note that this dish is yummy but doesn't transfer well to plates for serving, so you may want to serve it in the pan, with plenty of napkins available!

Chef's Notes

Zucchini Tartlets

Serves 8 to 10

Pastry:

1 - 8 ounce package cream cheese, softened

2 sticks butter, softened

2 cups flour – relax, this yields about 4 dozen tartlets

¼ cup grated Parmesan cheese, canned is best in this case

½ teaspoon Tony Chachere's Original Creole Seasoning

2 teaspoons cayenne pepper

To Prepare:

Combine all of the ingredients in a medium sized mixing bowl. Be sure to stir the mixture until smooth. Use a teaspoon to make balls of pastry dough about ¾ inch in diameter.

Filling:

4 cups coarsely grated zucchini

¼ cup olive oil

3 cloves garlic, minced

3 tablespoons oregano flakes

1 tablespoon basil flakes

1 tablespoon reduced salt

Topping:

2 cups shredded mozzarella cheese

½ cup grated Parmesan cheese, canned is best in this case

To Prepare:

Use the same procedure to prepare the filling as for the zucchini pizza in the previous recipe. You will need a small muffin pan, like those used for pecan tassies. Place a pastry ball into each place in the muffin tin and use your thumb or the larger end of a pestle to gently press the pastry to the bottom and sides of the pan, creating little pie crusts. Spoon the zucchini filling into each prepared pastry. Sprinkle Parmesan cheese on top of each tartlet, then repeat using grated mozzarella cheese to top them off. Bake in a pre-heated 350-degree oven for 30-35 minutes or until the tops are lightly golden. Depending on how thin you make the pastry, you can get as many as 4 dozen tartlets out of this recipe, with each tartlet low in carbohydrate content. These are time-consuming but make fabulous hot hors d'oeuvres for a party.

Chef's Notes

Cream of Asparagus Soup

Serves 6 generously

2 pounds fresh asparagus, tips removed and set aside, stalks cut into 1 inch long pieces

4 tablespoons butter

½ teaspoon freshly ground white pepper

1 clove garlic, minced

5 cups heavy chicken stock

1 pint heavy whipping cream

3 tablespoons lemon juice

12 large shrimp, peeled, de-veined and tails removed

Sour cream to garnish

To Prepare:

In a heavy stockpot, melt the butter over medium heat. Add the cut stalks of asparagus, white pepper and garlic. Sauté the asparagus until bright green and slightly tender, with care not to scorch the butter or the asparagus, about four minutes. Add the chicken stock and bring to a boil. Remove the pot from the stove and let it cool to room temperature. Next, it is very important for the asparagus and stock to cool sufficiently, as your blender will erupt when you try to liquefy the soup if it's too hot. This not only hurts, but it makes an awful mess to boot! Transfer the soup to a blender or a food processor and liquefy the asparagus stalks in the chicken stock. Pour the liquefied mixture back into the stockpot add the heavy cream and lemon juice and cover. Bring the soup to a boil and reduce the heat to low. Slowly simmer the soup, covered, for 30 minutes, stirring occasionally. Add the shrimp and the reserved asparagus tips, bring the soup back to a slow simmer and remove from the stove. Let the soup rest covered for about 15-20 minutes before serving. To serve, simply ladle the soup into bowls, trying to give each person two shrimp. Garnish with a dollop of sour cream if desired.

Heavy chicken stock is chicken stock that is concentrated. You can use canned stock but add 1 KNORR® chicken bouillon cube to each quart of canned stock for the right strength.

Chef's Notes

Exotic Cream of Mushroom Soup

Serves 6 to 8

1 pound fresh morel mushrooms

½ pound fresh chanterelle mushrooms

½ pound fresh oyster ear mushrooms

½ pound fresh porcini mushrooms

½ pound fresh shiitake mushrooms

1 stick butter

2 cloves garlic, minced

¼ teaspoon freshly ground white pepper

1 cup Cognac

2 KNORR® chicken bouillon cubes

2 quarts heavy whipping cream

1 quart half and half

Juice of one lemon

¼ teaspoon marjoram flakes

To Prepare:

In a large stockpot over high heat, melt the stick of butter. Add the mushrooms, one clove of minced garlic and half of the white pepper. Sauté the mushrooms until all of the liquids they purge dissipate, and the mushrooms begin to lightly brown. Quickly add the cognac and the bouillon. De-glaze the mushrooms for about two to three minutes. Reduce the heat to medium and add the heavy cream and the half and half. Add the remaining white pepper and the marjoram flakes. Bring the soup to a simmer, cover and reduce the heat to low. Let the soup simmer covered on low for about 45 minutes then add the lemon juice. Simmer covered for an additional 15 minutes then remove the covered pot from the stove and let it cool for about 15 minutes before serving. If morels or other exotic mushrooms are unavailable, you can substitute other types, or try dried exotic mushrooms; sometimes they are easier to find.

Chef's Notes

Lobster Bisque

Serves 4 to 6

Lobster tails, about 1½ pounds total; plus one claw
  per person, optional

6 Italian plumb tomatoes skinned, de-seeded and diced fine

2 cloves garlic, minced

½ teaspoon Tony Chachere's Original Creole Seasoning

2 cups Cognac

1 ½ cubes KNORR® chicken or fish bouillon

1 lemon, juiced and rind reserved

2 qt. heavy whipping cream

2 pinches of fresh ground white pepper

1 pinch of fresh ground black pepper

To Prepare:

In a large stockpot, combine lobster tails and claws in their shells with Cognac, garlic and pepper (white & black), Tony Chachere's Seasoning and bouillon. Add the lemon juice to the pot. Toss lemon rind in the pot, heat to medium-high, cover and boil for about four to five minutes or until the lobster is cooked. Now don't let this surprise you, but we're not going to throw anything away! Turn the stove off and remove the pot from the stove. Remove the lobster from the pot setting it aside in a bowl to cool and return the pot to the stove with the remaining liquids and lemon rind. Once the lobster is cool enough to handle, about five or six minutes, using a pair of kitchen shears, carefully extract the meat from the shell. Begin by cutting the shells on the underside of the tail at each edge then move on to the claws and even the legs if you used a whole lobster. Throw the empty shells back into the pot as you extract the meat from them. Leave the lobster meat that you have extracted from the shell in a bowl off to the side while you finish the bisque. The reason we don't throw the lobster right back in the pot is because we don't want to overcook the lobster. Now bring the fluids in the pot with the lobster shells and lemon rind back to a boil. Reduce the heat to a steady simmer and continue cooking until the liquids are reduced by half. Remove from heat, pour contents of the pot through a fine sieve into a bowl, reserving the stock. Wipe the pot out with a paper towel only to remove any shell shards or other debris that you don't want in the bisque. Return the Lobster stock to the pot and add diced tomatoes, bring to a slow simmer, add heavy cream, return to a slow simmer and cook for another 25 to 30 minutes. While the bisque is simmering using an electric blending stick blend through the simmering bisque to completely liquefy the diced tomatoes so the only lumps in your bisque will be lobster. Shred the tail meat coarsely and try to leave the claw meat intact to serve. Five minutes before the bisque is done add the shredded tail meat. Remove the bisque from the heat and let it rest for 10-15 minutes. At this time you can place the reserved lobster claws in a basket sieve, place the sieve over the bisque and cover so the claws become reheated from the steam of the bisque before serving. To serve, ladle the bisque into heated bowls and float a claw in the middle of each bowl. Incredible and pretty!!!

Chef's Notes

Tomato Soup alla Fiorentina

Serves 4

2 pounds Italian plumb tomatoes, skins removed, de-seeded and diced

4 tablespoons butter

1 clove garlic, minced

½ cup dry white wine

2 cubes KNORR® chicken bouillon

1 pint heavy whipping cream

1 tablespoon celery leaves, chopped

1 tablespoon fresh Italian parsley, chopped

1 shake nutmeg or 2-3 scratches grated fresh

White pepper to taste

To Prepare:

Begin by bringing a large stockpot of water to a boil. Immerse the tomatoes a few at a time in the boiling water for about one minute. This will loosen the skins, allowing you to skin them easily. When all of the tomatoes have been skinned cut them open, wash out all of the seeds, and dice them finely. Dump the boiling water and return the pot to the stove. Heat the pan to a medium-high heat and melt the butter. Add the garlic and tomatoes to the pot. Cook the tomatoes until they begin to sauce up, about five minutes. Add the white wine and the bouillon, reducing the heat to medium. Simmer for about ten more minutes. Add cream, nutmeg, celery leaves and Italian parsley. Reduce heat to low. Bring to a simmer again, cover and cook for another ten minutes before serving. Add white pepper to taste. If you prefer a smoother finish, use an electric blending stick to break up the tomato pieces.

Chef's Notes

Bacon Caesar Salad

Serves 2

1 head romaine lettuce, quartered and cut into 1 inch squares

½ cup freshly grated Parmesan cheese

4 slices lean thick cut bacon cut into ½ inch strips, browned but not crisp or crunchy, drippings reserved.

Dressing:

½ cup plain yogurt

2 teaspoons lemon juice

½ teaspoon black pepper, freshly ground

1 clove garlic, minced

2 tablespoons reserved bacon drippings

To Prepare:

Combine two tablespoons of the reserved drippings from the bacon with ½ cup of plain yogurt, two teaspoons of lemon juice, ½ teaspoon of freshly ground black pepper, and one clove of garlic, minced. Whisk all together until well combined.

Assembly:

Toss the lettuce, bacon and dressing together in a large mixing bowl until the greens are evenly coated with dressing. Sprinkle the Parmesan cheese over the top and serve.

Caesar Salad

Serves 2 to 4

1 head romaine lettuce quartered and cut into 1 inch squares

½ cup freshly grated Parmesan cheese

1 tablespoon small Caesar croutons

Dressing:

In a blender or food processor, combine ½ cup of olive oil, two cloves of garlic, ¾ teaspoon of freshly ground pepper, one teaspoon of anchovy paste, one egg and one tablespoon of lemon juice. Combine until the ingredients are liquefied and homogenous.

To Prepare:

Toss the lettuce, dressing and croutons together in a large mixing bowl, coating the greens well. Transfer to a serving plate and sprinkle Parmesan cheese over the top.

Remember: if you have been too generous with your carbohydrate intake for the day, eliminate the croutons. Sunflower seeds may be substituted for the croutons, and only have 1.5 grams of carbohydrate per tablespoon.

Chef's Notes

_____

_____

_____

_____

_____

_____

_____

_____

_____

_____

_____

Caesar Salad with a Greek Twist

Serves 1 to 2

1 head romaine lettuce quartered and cut into 1 inch squares

2 Italian plumb tomatoes, diced finely

½ cup feta cheese, crumbled

¼ cup ripe olives sliced

⅛ cup green olives sliced, optional, if you like

¼ cup artichoke hearts, preferably those packed in vinaigrette

⅛ cup olive oil

Creamy Caesar dressing, your brand of choice

½ cup freshly grated Parmesan cheese

To Prepare:

Combine all ingredients in a large salad bowl. Drizzle olive oil and creamy Caesar dressing over the top, and toss together, evenly coating the ingredients with the dressing. Garnish liberally with freshly grated Parmesan cheese.

Cantaloupe Cucumber & Shrimp Salad

Serves 4 to 6

1 pound frozen cocktail shrimp, defrosted, tails removed and chopped into coarse chunks

½ cantaloupe, rind removed and diced into small, ¼ inch cubes

1 cucumber, peeled and diced finely

1 tablespoon fresh dill chopped fine

1 clove garlic, minced

2 tablespoons rice wine vinegar

1 lemon, juiced

1 tablespoon honey

To Prepare:

In a mixing bowl, combine the diced cantaloupe, cucumber and shrimp. Add the remaining ingredients to the bowl and toss well. Place the salad in the refrigerator to chill for at least four hours, allowing the flavors to meld together. Serve in a salad bowl, or, when cutting the cantaloupe in half, use a paring knife and cut the melon transversely in half using triangular cuts to create a pinking-sheared effect to the remaining melon half. Then scoop out the seeds from the half you haven't diced, and use the melon as a bowl from which to serve. If the melon doesn't want to sit flat, simply cut a flat spot on the underside before filling, and it should sit up nicely like a bowl. Looks great on the table at summer gatherings, and the salad has a wonderfully refreshing flavor.

Chef's Notes

Chicken Mango Salad
with Yogurt Mustard Dressing

Serves 2

1 head iceberg lettuce, torn

1 mango peeled and cubed into ½ inch cubes

3 boneless skinless chicken breasts

Tony Chachere's Original Creole Seasoning to taste

3 tablespoons small croutons or 1 tablespoon sunflower seeds

Dressing:

1 cup plain yogurt

5 tablespoons lemon juice

3 tablespoons honey

5 tablespoons Dijon mustard

2 tablespoons olive oil

Dash cayenne pepper

Fresh ground black pepper to taste

To Prepare the Dressing:

Combine yogurt, lemon juice, honey, Dijon mustard, olive oil, cayenne pepper and black pepper in a two-cup measuring cup. Whisk ingredients together well.

To Prepare the Salad:

Sprinkle Tony's Original Creole Seasoning over the chicken to taste. Grill and cube the chicken into ½ inch to 1 inch pieces. Combine with lettuce, mango and croutons, add dressing, toss well and serve. Incredible!!!

*   Try mango yogurt for a sweeter taste, but remember to count the extra sugar and carbohydrates in the fruit.

Chef's Notes

Grilled Chicken Salad with Lemon Grass Dressing

Serves 2

3 boneless skinless chicken breasts

Lemon pepper to season the chicken breasts

1 head romaine lettuce quartered and cut into 1 inch pieces

1 ounce chevre cheese, crumbled; feta cheese may be substituted

½ cup pistachio nuts chopped very coarsely

Marinade:

½ cup lemon juice

2 cloves garlic, minced

½ teaspoon marjoram flakes

Dressing:

½ cup olive oil

⅓ cup lemon juice

2 cloves garlic, minced

3 tablespoons lemon grass chopped fine

2 teaspoons anchovy paste; Giovanni's Anchovy Paste is best

½ teaspoon freshly ground black pepper

To Prepare:

Marinade the chicken for six hours or overnight.

Assemble the lettuce, cheese and pistachio nuts in a large salad bowl. Combine all of the dressing ingredients in a blender and liquefy until all ingredients are well-combined, about one minute. Grill the marinated chicken and cut into ½ inch cubes. Toss the grilled cubed chicken together with the salad and dressing and serve. This salad has a wonderfully buttery taste, and is slightly warm due to the grilled chicken. Wonderfully light summer salad!!!

Chef's Notes

Grilled Salmon Caesar Salad

Serves 1

1 10-12 ounce filet of salmon

1 teaspoon Tony Chachere's Original Creole Seasoning, divided

1 head romaine lettuce quartered and cut into one inch pieces

½ cup fresh grated Parmesan cheese, divided

Fresh ground black pepper to taste

To Prepare:

Dress both sides of the salmon filet with Tony Chachere's Seasoning. Grill on each side for about five minutes, or until desired doneness. Place the cut romaine lettuce into a mixing bowl. Add Caesar salad dressing (your favorite brand or my recipe) in amount of your preference, as long as the lettuce is evenly coated. Add half of the Parmesan cheese and toss well. Place the tossed salad in a large serving dish and break the grilled salmon filet into bite-sized chunks, spreading it over the top. Garnish with the remaining Parmesan cheese and serve. You may add ¼ cup of Chow Mien noodles around the edge if desired, and if you have enough room for the carbs. Quick and very fulfilling!

Insalata di Pomodoro
Italian Tomato Salad

Serves 4 to 6

1 pound Italian plumb tomatoes, de-seeded and quartered

½ cup fresh basil, washed and cut, horizontally into ⅛ inch thick ribbons

2 cloves garlic, minced

⅓ cup red wine vinegar

½ cup extra virgin olive oil

1 tablespoon balsamic vinegar of good quality

Salt to taste

To Prepare:

Wash, quarter and de-seed the tomatoes. Wash and slice the basil leaves. In a large mixing bowl, combine all of the ingredients. Cover and chill in the refrigerator for 3 to four hours before serving. Stir the tomatoes occasionally to keep them coated in the dressing. This dish does not fare well if left to marinade overnight. Try serving this over slices of fresh mozzarella, the kind that comes packaged floating in whey. Incredibly good and refreshing!

Chef's Notes

Mediterranean Wilted Spinach

Serves 4

1 pound fresh baby spinach leaves washed, stems removed

1 cup fresh strawberries, topped and sliced

3 slices thick cut bacon, sliced into ⅛ inch thick ribbons

1 clove garlic, minced

1 tablespoon olive oil

1 teaspoon fresh coarsely ground black pepper

¼ cup of good quality balsamic vinegar

1 tablespoon honey

2 tablespoons toasted pine nuts

To Prepare:

In a non-stick skillet over medium low heat, stirring constantly, toast the pine nuts until lightly golden. Remove the toasted pine nuts from the skillet, setting them aside for later. Return the non-stick skillet to the stove and over medium-high heat fry the bacon until browned but not crunchy. Remove the bacon from the pan, reserving the drippings in the skillet and drain the bacon on paper toweling. Return the pan to the stove and reduce the heat to medium. Add minced garlic, olive oil, freshly ground black pepper, balsamic vinegar and honey. Bring this mixture to a boil and slightly reduce volume, by about ⅓. Remove from heat and let the dressing rest for about one minute. Pour the dressing over the prepared spinach sprinkle toasted pine nuts and bacon over the top and garnish with freshly sliced strawberries. This is a wonderful salad you will find refreshingly satisfying.

Chef's Notes

Parisian Salad with Lemon Pecan Dressing

Serves 1 to 2

1 heart of romaine lettuce quartered and cut into 1 inch pieces

½ cup escarole torn

½ cup radicchio torn

8 ounces prosciutto sliced into ½ inch wide ribbons

2 hard boiled eggs diced

1 Italian plumb tomato diced finely

2 ounces gruyere cheese sliced into shavings

Dressing:

½ cup olive oil

¼ cup pecan pieces

2 anchovy filets

1 clove garlic, minced

¼ cup lemon juice

2 tablespoons lemon grass chopped finely

To Prepare:

Heat the olive oil over low heat. Add the pecan pieces, sauté for two to three minutes. Remove from heat. Using a mortar and pestle, combine one heaping teaspoon of the sautéed pecan pieces and one tablespoon of the olive oil from the pan with the anchovy filets and minced garlic and grind into a paste. Return the paste to the pan with remaining oil and whisk together until well combined. Add the lemon juice and fresh ground black pepper to taste. Pour the dressing over the salad and toss. Garnish with shaved cheese, diced egg and prosciutto ribbons. This salad is both beautiful and delicious.

Parmesan Salad

Serves 1 to 2

1 head romaine lettuce quartered and cut into 1 inch squares

2 ounces Parmesan cheese, shaved into slivers

2 Italian plumb tomatoes, diced finely

Dressing:

½ cup olive oil

½ cup Parmesan cheese, canned, pre-grated in this case

1 ½ cloves garlic, minced

⅓ cup red wine vinegar

1 teaspoon freshly ground black pepper

1 tablespoon honey

To Prepare:

Whisk together all of the dressing ingredients. Place lettuce and diced tomato in a large mixing bowl. Toss salad with the dressing, sprinkle Parmesan slivers over the top and serve.

Chef's Notes

_____

_____

_____

_____

_____

_____

_____

_____

_____

_____

Ranch Salad

Serves 2

1 head iceberg lettuce, torn

2-3 Italian plumb tomatoes, diced finely

3 scallions, whites diced finely; greens sliced thin

4 slices thick cut bacon sliced into ½ strips and fried until crispy but chewy, not crunchy

1 cup Cheddar jack cheese grated

⅓ to ½ cup of ranch dressing.

To Prepare:

Toss all of the ingredients above together making sure to evenly coat the lettuce and serve. Easy to prepare, and exceptionally good with recipe for Deviled Crab Cakes on page 96.

Roast Duck Salad with Raspberry Vinaigrette Suzanne

Serves 2 to 4

1 duck roasted, pulled from the bone and torn

1 medium sweet onion quartered

1 rib celery

1 sprig fresh rosemary

1 head Boston lettuce torn

¾ cup radicchio shredded

1 heart of romaine lettuce torn

½ cup pistachio nut pieces

Dressing:

½ cup white wine vinegar

1 cup fresh frozen raspberries

1 tablespoon balsamic vinegar

1 tablespoon Dijon mustard

1 tablespoon olive oil

2 teaspoons SPLENDA™ Granular

1 clove garlic

To Prepare:

Advice: roast the duck the day before, completing all but the dressing and assembly.

Defrost and wash the duck well. Stuff the cavity with one sweet onion, one rib of celery and one sprig of rosemary. Place the duck in a crock-pot and roast on high until meat is nearly falling off the bone, about five to six hours. When done, remove the duck from the crock-pot and let it cool on a rack. When cool, remove the meat from the bone and tear into bite-size pieces. Set the pulled duck aside until it's time to assemble the salad.

In a blender, combine all of the ingredients for the dressing and blend until liquefied. Set the dressing aside. In a large salad bowl, combine the torn Boston, romaine and radicchio lettuces. Add the pulled duck and pistachio nut pieces. Pour the dressing over the salad and toss well, making sure that all the ingredients are well coated before serving. This salad has a wonderfully buttery, explosive flavor; you'll love it!

Chef's Notes

Salade Niçoise

Serves 2

2 hearts of romaine lettuce quartered and cut into 1 inch squares

2 cans of tuna drained. solid white albacore packed in water
is the best

½ cup marinated artichoke hearts

3 large medium boiled eggs quartered

2 Italian plumb tomatoes diced

1 cup green beans, cooked but still crisp, chilled

1 small red potato cooked, peeled and cubed coarsely, if you have
not had any carbohydrates for the day!

8 anchovy filets, packed in olive oil

½ cup feta or chevre cheese crumbled

Dressing:

⅓ cup olive oil

Juice of one lemon (should equal ⅓ cup of lemon juice)

2 cloves garlic, minced

2 teaspoons fresh ground black pepper

1 teaspoon anchovy paste, Giovanni's is the best

To Prepare:

Whisk together all of the dressing ingredients in a small bowl
and set aside for five minutes.

In a large bowl, combine the lettuce, tuna, tomatoes, green beans,
artichoke hearts, cubed potato and cheese. Pour the dressing over
the top and toss together well, making sure to evenly coat the salad
with the dressing. Arrange the egg quarters around the outside edges
of the salad. Place anchovies in a star-like formation over the top of
the salad, and serve. This salad is both beautiful and delicious,
enough for two.

Chef's Notes

Seven Layer Salad

Serves 6 to 8

This salad is truly an American classic. However I must dedicate this recipe to my mother-in-law, as she is certainly the master of this mouthwatering favorite of mine. Each ingredient equals a layer in this salad, hence the name and seven ingredients. This salad is great with ribs, steaks, and any grilled food. The original recipe calls for sugar in the dressing, but as we all know sugar is poison in this diet, so I cleverly substituted SPLENDA™ Granular, a sugar byproduct without a funky aftertaste and only a trace of glucose. I think this salad will become your favorite too.

1 head iceberg lettuce, torn into small pieces

½ large Bermuda onion, diced

4 green onions; whites diced, greens sliced into ringlets

1 ½ cups mayonnaise mixed with ½ cup SPLENDA™ Granular

1 ½ cups frozen green peas, thawed

2 cups marble Cheddar cheese

1 pound thick-sliced bacon cut into ½ inch wide strips, browned
    but not crunchy.

To Prepare:

Assemble the ingredients in order listed above. When it comes to the dressing layer, use a rubber spatula to smooth the dressing over the greens, almost like icing a cake, then proceed to the next layer. Once assembled, let the salad rest undisturbed. Don't let people help themselves early, because once this salad is scooped, it sweats and gets runny. It is best if you let the salad rest overnight in the refrigerator before serving. Serves 6-8 depending on how big a salad eating crowd you feed. I could make a meal of the whole thing myself… it's so good!

Chef's Notes

Smoked Turkey and Wild Rice Salad

Serves 2

12 ounces smoked turkey, cut into ½ inch cubes

½ cup wild rice, prepared as below

2 celery stalks, split and sliced thin

1 cup seedless red grapes cut into half, lengthwise

3 scallions diced finely

1 Granny Smith apple cored and cubed into ½ inch cubes

Dressing:

1 cup plain yogurt, for less fat use yogurt made from
       skimmed milk

3 tablespoons honey

2 tablespoons lemon juice

1 tablespoon olive oil

2 teaspoons black pepper

⅛ teaspoon cayenne pepper

To Prepare:

In a two cup measuring cup, combine the dressing ingredients with a whisk. Whisk until smooth and set aside.

In a large bowl, combine rice, turkey, grapes, celery, scallions and Granny Smith apples. Add the dressing, combine well to coat evenly. This can be served immediately or covered and chilled overnight to infuse all of the flavors.

Makes a great lunch option, or a good foundation for other sides for dinner.

Method for rice:

Wash the wild rice in a mesh sieve, then transfer it to a heavy sauce pan. Add two cups water and one cube KNORR® chicken bouillon. Bring to a boil, then reduce to a simmer. Cover the pan and simmer for one hour or until the rice is tender. When done, the rice grains should be splitting open a little. Drain off any excess liquid and remove from the stove to cool to room temperature. This may be prepared days ahead.

Chef's Notes

Three Bean Tuna Salad alla Modena

Serves 2 as a main dish for lunch

1 ½ cups fresh or frozen green beans

1 ½ cups fresh or frozen Italian flat beans

1 ½ cups canned wax beans, rinsed and drained

2 cans solid white albacore tuna packed in water, drained

½ cup extra virgin olive oil

½ cup good quality balsamic vinegar

2 cloves garlic, minced

2 teaspoons freshly ground black pepper

4 Italian plumb tomatoes, diced medium

1 cup feta cheese, crumbled

To Prepare:

Fresh beans are best but frozen will do. Boil the green beans and flat beans until tender but still crisp, about four to five minutes, drain and set aside to cool. Rinse and drain the wax beans. In a large mixing bowl, combine the beans with the remaining ingredients and stir well. Chill the salad thoroughly before serving, about three to four hours. The salad can also be prepared and chilled the night before, but the flavor of the fish will be more pronounced. Either way, this is a delightful salad and even makes a great main dish on warm days.

Note: In Modena, this salad is traditionally prepared with slivered Parmesan Reggiano cheese instead of feta. Substituting feta cheese gives the salad more bang, but if you're striving for authenticity, use ½ cup of slivered Parmegianno Reggiano instead. Salt is optional as the cheese lends salt to the salad naturally.

Chef's Notes

Tuna Fish Salad Italian Style

Serves 1 to 2

1 head iceberg lettuce torn

3 Italian plumb tomatoes diced medium to fine

2 cans solid white albacore tuna in spring water drained

2 tablespoons small croutons

¼ cup artichoke hearts in olive oil and vinegar drained

⅔ cup Parmesan cheese grated; canned pre-grated is best in this case, believe it or not, because it coats better

Dressing:

½ cup olive oil

⅓ cup red wine vinegar

1 tablespoon garlic powder

½ teaspoon salt

2 tablespoons fresh ground black pepper

To Prepare:

Tear the lettuce into nice bite-sized pieces. Toss the lettuce, tomatoes, tuna and artichoke hearts with dressing. Add the Parmesan cheese and toss again. Garnish the salad with the small croutons. This salad is both incredible in taste and filling.

Chef's Notes

Turkey Waldorf Salad

Serves 1 to 2

12 ounces turkey cubed into ¼ inch cubes

1 Granny Smith apple, cubed into ¼ inch cubes

½ head of iceberg lettuce torn

1 cup red seedless grapes cut in half

½ cup walnut halves

Dressing:

8 ounces plain low fat yogurt

¼ cup lemon juice

3 tablespoons honey

½ teaspoon garlic powder

Dash of cayenne pepper

To Prepare:

In a large salad bowl, combine the cubed turkey, Granny Smith apple, iceberg lettuce, seedless grapes and walnuts. In a two cup measuring cup, combine the yogurt, lemon juice, honey, garlic powder and cayenne pepper; whisk together until smooth. Pour the dressing over the top of the salad and toss well to evenly coat the salad with dressing. This is a great lunch item and is plenty for two people. The tartness of the Granny Smith apple really gives this salad a spark.

For extra zip, add ⅛ cup of golden raisins and ⅛ cup of feta cheese sprinkled over the top.

You can buy the turkey in the deli section of your grocery store. Ask the counter person to slice the turkey into a ¼ inch thick slice, like a ham steak. Cut the sliced turkey into equal cubes for an easier approach.

Chef's Notes

Sandwiches

Sandwiches

Sandwiches for lunch are often missed by those of us on low-carb diets. Sure, you can make a lettuce burrito with cold cuts and some really good mustard or horseradish sauce, but without bread, once and a while you do get a little bored. Again, thanks to the expanding market for low-carb foods, other solutions are now available. There are companies that sell bread mixes that are low-carb and taste good, and other companies that produce low-carb bread already baked... but they are hard to find. My favorite low-carb company, **LowCarb Success,** makes a pizza dough mix that I have used to make excellent sandwich wraps. The wraps can be made ahead on the weekend, and reserved for use over your work week.

Sandwich Wraps

1 package of **LowCarb Success** Pizza Crust mix and yeast packet

2 cups warm water

¼ cup olive oil

To Prepare:

Mix the ingredients together well with a rubber spatula. Coat your hands with olive oil, then roll the dough into a long roll, like French bread, about 1½ inches in diameter. Cut the roll into pieces about 1½ to 2 inches long. Roll the sections into balls, cover them with a cloth and set them aside to rest in a warm place for 20 minutes. Using soy flour, dust the work surface to prevent sticking and roll the balls out into tortillas. Heat a heavy skillet to a medium setting add enough olive oil to the skillet to lightly cover the bottom and fry each tortilla on both sides, about two to three minutes each side or until kissed with a golden color. Stack them just like tortillas and place in a plastic bag to preserve freshness. For a little variation in flavor try adding one tablespoon of caraway seed to the mix for a rye taste.

Aside from bread itself, you must be vigilant about the carbohydrate content of toppings. Remember: cold cuts are generally cured, hence sugar is added. Ham is the most commonly cured meat you will find in the deli case. Smoked meats are also commonly cured with sugar. Be careful when buying lunchmeats; they may not be as low-carb as you think.

The next thing to remember about a good sandwich is to use really good condiments. My favorite company in this category has been making mustards and horseradish for more than 100 years. The name is **Woeber's**. They have a vast variety of really high quality mustards and sandwich spreads that will perk up any sandwich – or any salad for that matter.

The Lettuce Burrito

This is the original low-carb answer to a sandwich. While you might expect it to taste bland, it really needn't be dull.

Begin by removing the outer leaves of a head of iceberg lettuce, trying to keep them intact. I use two leaves fit together like a big bowl, then add a layer of lunchmeat topped with a really good mustard like **Woeber's Jalapeno Mustard,** plus some cheese. With turkey, I like to start with lettuce leaves, layer on a slice of turkey, next some **Woeber's Horseradish Sauce,** and then some fresh ground black pepper corns, followed by provolone cheese. Once you're done layering your Dagwood sandwich to perfection, simply fold the edges of the lettuce bowl over the contents, or roll it all up like a big lettuce burrito. You can use any sturdy lettuce that you like; I find iceberg to be the sturdiest.

Leaves of Boston lettuce are not only delicious but they make tidy little cups that are perfect for salad sandwiches like Tuna Salad. I use a can of solid white albacore tuna packed in spring water, well drained. Then I dice up two or three sweet pickles, combine the tuna fish and the pickles, and add a heaping soup spoon of mayonnaise.

Be adventuresome when you buy sandwich supplies. Take some time to look at condiments you never normally purchase. You never know what tasty treasure you may find out there. A good example would be **Woeber's Cranberry Horseradish Sauce.** Try it with a slice of ham and some jalapeno jack cheese: WOW!

Main Entrees

Main Entrees

An important note: Throughout these recipes I have used a variety of wines, Champagne, cordials and liquors. Please keep in mind that these are all forms of alcohol. Alcohol is flammable. If you are using a gas stove or cooking by open flame, always remove the pan from the source of the flame before adding the alcohol to the pan. This will help to prevent a flash fire. A flash fire caused by igniting alcohol can burn either you or your kitchen. Please be safe when cooking with alcohol.

For the new cook, you will also find a dictionary of cooking terms at the back of the book, as well as a chart to help you count the carbohydrates in various foods.

Ahi Ruby with Ginger Pesto

Serves 2

2 filets of ahi about 1½ inches thick, 10 - 12 ounces each

1 tablespoon grapeseed oil

1 teaspoon grated ginger root

1 clove garlic, minced

Onion salt to taste

Sliced pickled ginger and wasabi to garnish

To Prepare:

Place the ahi filet in a sealable bag with grapeseed oil, grated ginger root and minced garlic. Marinade in the refrigerator for a minimum of 30 minutes but no longer than one hour. When ready to cook, heat a non-stick skillet over medium-high heat. Remove the filet from the bag and dust with onion salt to taste. Pour the liquids from the sealable bag into the skillet and add the seasoned ahi filet. Sear the ahi filet on each side until done.

"Ruby" refers to the fact that the filet is served rare: red (but warm) in the center. If you don't like the idea of eating rare fish you may cook it longer.

When done, remove the filet from the skillet. Plate it and place a dollop of the ginger pesto over the top. Garnish with three slices of pickled gingerroot and a piece of wasabi.

Ginger Pesto

2 tablespoons butter

1 tablespoon ground ginger, Spice World brand

2 teaspoons lemon juice

1 clove garlic, minced

Fresh ground white pepper to taste

To Prepare:

In a small bowl, combine the softened butter, ginger, garlic, and pepper by beating together with a spoon. Stir in the lemon juice slowly drizzling it into the butter mixture. The pesto should be similar in consistency to mayonnaise.

Chef's Notes

_____

_____

_____

_____

_____

_____

_____

_____

_____

_____

Bourbon Barbecued Ribs

Serves 4

5 pounds boneless lean country pork ribs

Barbecue sauce of your choice

Marinade:

1 cup Bourbon

1 cup Italian vinaigrette dressing

To Prepare:

Marinade for one day in the refrigerator agitating every couple of hours. Before grilling, place ribs in aluminum foil, making packets containing the ribs and marinade. Grill in packets for one hour, turning about every 12-15 minutes. After one hour of grilling, peel back the top of the packets and place ribs directly on the grill. Brush on your favorite barbecue sauce as you finish grilling the ribs, coating all sides. If your barbecue sauce doesn't have bourbon in it, add a tablespoon or two to get the most bang out of the sauce. Try serving these with the Seven Layer Salad recipe (page 72) or my Ranch Salad recipe (page 68).

Braised Sea Scallops with Peppers

Serves 1 to 2

12-16 large sea scallops

2 shallots, diced finely

1 large clove of garlic, minced

2 large red bell peppers de-seeded, sliced julienne ⅛ inch wide

¼ cup white zinfandel wine or mead, a wine made from honey

2 tablespoons sweet unsalted butter

To Prepare:

In a medium sauté pan, melt the butter gently over low heat. Add shallots and sauté until transparent, about two minutes. Add scallops and increase heat to high. When the scallops begin to sear, turn them over and add red bell peppers over the scallops. When the scallops are seared on both sides, add the wine and garlic. Reduce heat to medium-high and allow all ingredients to simmer for about two more minutes, stirring frequently. To serve, plate and drizzle any remaining fluids over the top before serving. Delicious!

* Mead, a wine made from honey, may be used in place of zinfandel if you prefer a sweeter finish to the sauce.

Chef's Notes

Cajun Pan Seared Golden Tilapia

Serves 1

1 filet golden tilapia

2 tablespoons butter

Tony Chachere's Original Creole Seasoning

1 tablespoon lemon juice

To Prepare:

Over medium-high heat, melt the butter in a non-stick skillet. Generously sprinkle Tony Chachere's Seasoning over the fish. Pan-fry the filet for about four to five minutes on each side, or until the edges are lightly crisp and the sides are golden. Pour the lemon juice over the filet. When the juice has evaporated in the pan, it's ready to serve. This dish is pungently delicious and has almost no carbohydrates!

*This recipe is yummy with boneless skinless chicken breast and pork medallions too! Simply increase the cooking time when browning the meat as both chicken and pork should be cooked thoroughly.

Chicken Marsala

Serves 6

6 boneless skinless chicken breasts

2 tablespoons butter

1 clove garlic, minced

1 cube KNORR® chicken bouillon

½ cup marsala wine (dry)

½ cup orange juice

1 pint heavy whipping cream

To Prepare:

In a heavy non-stick skillet, melt the butter over medium-high heat. Add the minced garlic and place the chicken in the skillet. Sear the chicken until golden brown on each side. Add the marsala, orange juice and bouillon to the skillet, essentially de-glazing the chicken. Bring the liquids to a boil. When the liquids are reduced by ¾ (about 10-15 minutes) remove the chicken from the skillet and set aside.

Continue reducing the liquids to cords. "Reducing to cords" is when the liquid caramelizes to a state where scraping a spoon through the bubbling liquid leaves a clean sweep behind the spoon for a few seconds after it passes.

Reduce heat to medium and add the cream. Bring the liquids back to a vigorous simmer, and let the cream reduce a little too, about five minutes. Return the chicken to the sauce and thoroughly heat through before serving, about four minutes.

Chef's Notes

_____

_____

_____

_____

_____

_____

_____

_____

_____

_____

_____

_____

Cod Filet in Brie Velouté Sauce

Serves 1

1 large filet of cod fish

1 shallot finely chopped or minced

2 tablespoons butter

½ cup heavy whipping cream

½ cube KNORR® chicken or fish bouillon

2 ounces brie cheese, crust removed

6 large shrimp, peeled, de-veined and tails removed

To Prepare:

In a non-stick skillet, melt the butter, add the minced shallot, and sauté gently over medium heat until the shallots are warmed through well, about one minute. Add the filet of cod, cooking on one side for about two to three minutes. Turn the filet over and add the cream, brie and bouillon. Gently agitate the contents of the skillet together with a spatula to dissolve the cheese and bouillon. When the sauce has formed and is smooth add the shrimp and cook until just done, about two minutes. When done, plate the fish filet to a dish with sides that retain the sauce. Spoon the shrimp and sauce over the top of the filet and serve. YUM!

* Believe it or not, you can substitute chicken for the fish in this recipe. Simply sauté the chicken longer, add a couple more shrimp and a dash of cayenne pepper. If you can find it in your area, try KNORR® chicken bouillon. It is usually found in the soup aisle but may also be found in the Mexican food section and makes a fantastic cream sauce!

Cod à la Meuniere

Serves 2

2 large cod filets (trout is a great substitute with this dish)

½ cup flour

4 tablespoons butter

Juice of one lemon

Fresh ground black pepper to taste

To Prepare:

In a non-stick pan, melt the butter over medium-high heat. Dredge the filets in flour lightly. Pan-fry the filets in the melted butter, turning filets only once when golden. When both sides are golden, remove the fish from the pan, placing the filet on a serving plate. Add the lemon juice to the pan drippings. Cook the mixture until a sauce forms about two to three minutes. Pour the sauce over the filets and serve.

Chef's Notes

Coquilles Saint Jacques

Serves 1 to 2

1 pound giant sea scallops

⅛ cup minced shallots

½ cup heavy whipping cream

4 ounces Monterey jack cheese cut into cubes or shredded

4-5 turns fresh ground white pepper, 2 dashes pre-ground

1 shot Cognac; quality is relative: the better the Cognac, the better
the sauce

1 tablespoon butter

½ cube KNORR® fish bouillon

To Prepare:

In a heavy saucepan over high heat, melt the butter. Add scallops
and sauté until they purge their liquids, about one or two minutes.
Remove the scallops and set them aside. Add the Cognac, pepper,
shallots and cook until the liquid reduces by ¾. Reduce the heat to
low and add the cream. When a slow simmer starts, add the cheese,
stirring constantly as it melts. When the sauce is smooth, remove
the pan from the heat. Spoon scallops into two small oven-safe chaff-
ing dishes or shallow oven-safe bowls. Pour in the sauce, dividing it
evenly over the scallops in the dishes, and place them in the broiler.
Broil the scallops in the cream sauce until lightly spotted golden,
about three to five minutes, depending on your broiler, and serve.

Delicious as a main dish, or serve as hors d'oeuvres using large
scallop shells or small custard cups in place of the larger cooking
vessels. Place three scallops in each shell or custard cup, cover with
cream sauce, and broil the same way.

Chef's Notes

Deviled Crab Cakes

Serves 2

1 can lump crab meat, 6 ounces

1 can white crab meat, 6 ounces

1 egg

1 tablespoon fresh ground extra hot horseradish, Woeber's brand

1 tablespoon mayonnaise, heaping

¼ teaspoon Tony Chachere's Original Creole Seasoning or
    2 pinches of cayenne pepper

3 green onions, white minced, greens cut into thin ringlets

1 ½ tablespoons whole kernel corn

2 chipotle peppers packed in adobo sauce, chopped coarsely.
    HERDEZ® brand is recommended for the natural smoked
    flavor

Progresso Italian Bread Crumbs for breading

2 tablespoons butter and 2 tablespoons olive oil for frying

To Prepare:

Using a spoon, gently combine all ingredients together except the bread crumbs. Separate the mixture into six equally sized balls. Very gently pat each ball into a patty. You're shooting for thick mini hamburger cakes about ³/₄ inch to 1 inch thick each. Spread about ½ cup of Progresso Italian Bread Crumbs on a paper plate and gently cover each patty with crumbs. Be careful not to work the bread crumbs into the crab cakes; as this will make them too doughy. Melt two tablespoons of butter and two tablespoons of olive oil together in a non-stick pan over low to medium heat. Gently place the crab cakes into the pan. Pan-fry until golden on each side. Avoid turning the cakes too frequently to avoid breaking them up. Finish time is approximately eight to ten minutes. These are wonderful and best served with Ranch Salad on page 68. If you take my recommendation for the salad, try reserving the bacon drippings from the bacon you prepared for the salad. Add olive oil to the drippings, and pan-fry the crab cakes in this mixture. Delicious!

Remember: fat doesn't count, as long as it's a natural fat!

Chef's Notes

Enchiladas Con Camarones in Salsa Verde
Shrimp Enchiladas with Green Sauce

Serves 2

¾ pound jumbo shrimp peeled, de-veined and cubed

1 cod loin, about 6 ounces

1 tablespoon olive oil

½ teaspoon cumin ground

2 cloves garlic, minced

1 chipotle pepper in adobo sauce diced fine; HERDEZ® brand is recommended for the natural smoked flavor

1 Italian plumb tomato, peeled, de-seeded and diced

2 tablespoons black beans, rinsed and drained; LA PREFERIDA® brand is suggested

2 green onions, whites chopped fine, greens cut into ringlets

1 cup shredded Monterey jack cheese, divided

½ cup sour cream

8 corn tortillas brushed with olive oil

Salsa Verde:

1 can, 7 ounces HERDEZ® brand Salsa Verde

½ cup sour cream

1 clove garlic, minced

1 cube KNORR® chicken bouillon

¼ cup lime juice

Green habanero sauce to taste

To Prepare:

In a non-stick skillet, heat the olive oil over medium-high heat. Add the cod loin, cumin and garlic. Sauté together for about two minutes. Add the shrimp. Sauté for another two minutes. Remove the fish and shrimp from the pan, and set aside in a mixing bowl. Add the chipotle pepper, diced tomato and green onions to the pan and sauté together for another two minutes. Remove the skillet from the stove and add the sautéed vegetables to the fish and shrimp in the mixing bowl. Fold the cheese and sour cream into the fish and shrimp mixture. Heat the tortillas brushed with olive oil on high in a microwave for about 45 seconds, or just until they are pliable. Add about two heaping spoonfuls of the filling into the middle of each of the tortillas and roll them up. Place four enchiladas on each plate. Meanwhile, combine all of the ingredients for the salsa verde in the same pan you used to prepare the fish and shrimp mixture, and bring to a simmer. Remove the sauce from the stove and ladle it over the enchiladas. Garnish the tops of the enchiladas with the rest of the Monterey jack cheese and place the enchiladas in the microwave on high for an additional three minutes or until the cheese on top melts. You can also broil the enchiladas to melt the cheese if you're using oven-safe dinnerware. Serve right away, while they're still hot. This is delicious, and an easy meal for two.

Chef's Notes

Enchiladas de Pescado de Cancun

Serves 1

1 filet golden tilapia

1 tablespoon butter

1 teaspoon olive oil

1 teaspoon Tony Chachere's Original Creole Seasoning, divided

1 teaspoon cumin, ground, divided

2 cloves of garlic, minced

10 large pre-cooked shrimp, coarsely diced

2 scallions, diced

1 chipotle pepper packed in adobo sauce, diced. HERDEZ® brand
is recommended for the natural smoked flavor

2 tablespoons black beans rinsed and drained. LA PREFERIDA®
brand is suggested

³⁄₄ cup colby jack cheese, shredded, divided

4 white corn tortillas

Olive oil to drizzle

Sauce:

2 cups water

1 cube KNORR® chicken bouillon

3 soupspoons mole; DOÑA MARÍA® brand preferred

To Prepare:

In a non-stick skillet, melt butter with olive oil over high heat.
Sprinkle half of the Tony Chachere's Seasoning and half of the cumin
on each side of the tilapia filet and fry in the skillet until golden on
each side. Remove the tilapia filet from the pan and set aside. Quickly
add minced garlic and coarsely diced shrimp to the pan and stir-fry
together for about one to two minutes, just long enough to infuse
the shrimp with the garlic. When done, remove shrimp from skillet,
place in a bowl, crumble the tilapia filet into the bowl, add green
onions, diced chipotle pepper, ½ cup of colby jack cheese and gently combine. Drizzle olive oil over the tortillas lightly and rub together to thoroughly cover each tortilla lightly with oil. Microwave
on high for about one minute, long enough to make them pliable.
Evenly divide the fish and shrimp mixture between the four tortillas
and roll into an enchilada. Place into a baking dish or plate, seam
side down.

To prepare the sauce, combine: water, mole and bouillon in a saucepan. Bring to a boil, reduce heat to simmer until thickened to a gravy. Spoon the sauce over the enchiladas, sprinkle ¼ cup of colby jack cheese over the top of the enchiladas and microwave on high until cheese is melted, about three minutes. To garnish, dollop sour cream over the top. These are delicious and filling.

Chef's Notes

_____

_____

_____

_____

_____

_____

_____

_____

_____

_____

_____

_____

Fiesta Salmon

Serves 1

One filet of salmon, 10-12 ounces

Sauce:

1 tablespoon butter

½ cup tomato juice

2 Italian plumb tomatoes, de-seeded and diced

¼ red bell pepper, de-seeded and diced

½ medium onion, diced

1 clove garlic, minced

½ cube KNORR® chicken bouillon

⅓ cup lime juice

1 teaspoon ground cumin

One dash cayenne pepper

1 teaspoon jalepeno green salsa

One or two slices pepper jack cheese

To Prepare:

In a non-stick skillet, melt the butter over medium-high heat. Add diced tomatoes, onions and red pepper. Sauté together until the onions are transparent, about two or three minutes. Add remaining ingredients, and bring the contents of the skillet to a simmer. Add the salmon. Turn the salmon over after it is cooked half through, another two or three minutes. Simmer to cook the other side. Place a slice of pepper jack cheese on top of the salmon, cover the skillet and remove from heat. When the cheese has melted, it's ready to serve.

* Boneless skinless chicken breast makes a great substitute in this recipe. Just remember to cook the chicken longer.

Chef's Notes

Fishkabob

Serves 2

1 ½ to 2 pounds monkfish, membrane removed, cubed into
     1 to 1½ inch cubes

1 large red Bermuda onion, quartered

2 large yellow bell peppers, de-seeded and cut into
     1½ inch squares

2 large red bell peppers de-seeded and cut into 1½ inch squares

Thick cut bacon, cut into 1 inch pieces. You will need one piece of
     bacon per piece of fish

Marinade:

1 heaping tablespoon of each of the following: black bean sauce, hoisin sauce, ground ginger and honey mixed well. Place the cubes of monkfish in a sealable bag with the marinade. Place the bag in the refrigerator and allow the fish to marinade for at least three hours.

To Prepare:

If you have metal skewers, they're perfect; if not, use bamboo skewers that you have soaked in water for about 20 minutes. When building a kabob of any type, always begin and end with a vegetable that will hold up through grilling, like an onion. Always pierce the convex surface of a vegetable first so that it creates a cup for the meat that you are putting on behind it.

Start with a piece of red onion followed by a cube of monkfish, a slice of bacon, a piece of pepper, followed by another cube of monkfish, another slice of bacon and a piece of onion. Keep repeating the process until all of the ingredients have been used.

You will end up with about four kabobs. Use the marinade in the bag for basting as you grill the kabobs over a low flame. The kabobs will get a little charred on the edges before they are done. When the bacon is cooked, the monkfish will certainly be done, and the kabobs are then ready to serve.

Chef's Notes

Frittati

The next four recipes are great entrée alternatives. Frittati are one of the oldest and most versatile dishes in Italian cuisine. The great thing about a frittata is that it can be served for breakfast, lunch or dinner. They are the Italian version of the famed French quiche – but without the carbohydrates form the crust that the French traditionally use.

Frittata di Gamberi alla Fiorentina
Shrimp Frittata Florentine Style

Serves 1 to 2

4 eggs, well beaten

¼ cup heavy whipping cream

1 dozen large shrimp, de-veined, shelled and tails removed

1 Italian plumb tomato, de-seeded and diced

2 scallions, sliced finely

1 clove garlic, minced

¼ pound provolone cheese, sliced thin

2 tablespoons butter

To Prepare:

In a mixing bowl, combine the eggs and cream and whip until frothy. In a non-stick skillet over medium heat, melt the butter. Add the whipped eggs and cream. Using a wooden spoon, stir the bottom of the skillet gently. When the eggs begin to get body, add the shrimp, plumb tomato, scallions, garlic and a couple of slices of provolone cheese broken into pieces, stirring them gently into the surface of the coagulating egg mixture. Try not to push the added ingredients to the bottom of the skillet to avoid scorching. Reduce the heat to low and cover. Let the frittata steam in the covered skillet to set the eggs, about three to four minutes. Place the remaining provolone cheese over the top and cover once again for about one or two minutes. When the cheese has melted, the frittata is ready to serve. Gently agitate the skillet, holding it at a 45-degree angle and carefully slip the frittata in one piece onto the serving plate. Quick and easy dinner and even good for breakfast. Try combining other vegetables and meats for a choice of breakfast entrees.

Chef's Notes

Frittata Lorraine

Serves 2

6 eggs whipped until frothy

4 tablespoons heavy whipping cream

6 slices thick cut lean bacon sliced into $\frac{1}{4}$ inch wide strips,
    browned but not crisp

$\frac{3}{4}$ cup Swiss cheese grated

2 tablespoons butter

To Prepare:

In a mixing bowl, combine the eggs and cream and whip until frothy. In a non-stick skillet over medium heat, melt the butter. Add the whipped eggs and cream. Using a wooden spoon, stir the bottom of the skillet gently. When the eggs begin to get body, add the bacon and $\frac{1}{2}$ cup of the grated Swiss cheese, stirring them gently into the surface of the coagulating egg mixture. Try not to push the bacon to the bottom of the skillet to avoid scorching. Reduce the heat to low and cover. Let the frittata steam in the covered skillet to set the eggs, about three to four minutes. Sprinkle the remaining grated Swiss cheese over the top and cover once again for about one or two minutes. When the cheese has melted, the frittata is ready to serve. Gently agitate the skillet, holding it at a 45-degree angle and carefully slip the frittata in one piece onto the serving plate.

Frittata alla Margherita

Serves 2

6 eggs whipped until frothy

2 tablespoons heavy whipping cream

2 Italian plumb tomatoes de-seeded and diced fine

1 clove garlic, minced

4 leaves basil, sliced into thin ribbons

4 fresh mushrooms, sliced thin

$\frac{1}{4}$ cup mozzarella cheese, shredded

1 tablespoon butter

To Prepare:

In a mixing bowl, combine the eggs and cream and whip until frothy. In a non-stick skillet over medium heat melt the butter. Add the whipped eggs and cream. Using a wooden spoon, stir the bottom of the skillet gently. When the eggs begin to get body, add the tomatoes, garlic, basil and mushrooms, stirring them gently into the surface of the coagulating egg mixture. Try not to push any of these ingredients to the bottom of the skillet to avoid scorching them. Reduce the heat to low and cover. Let the frittata steam in the covered skillet to set the eggs, about three to four minutes. Sprinkle the shredded mozzarella cheese over the top and cover once again. When the cheese has melted the frittata is ready to serve. Gently agitate the skillet, holding it at a 45-degree angle and carefully slip the frittata in one piece onto the serving plate.

Chef's Notes

Frittata di Spinaci

Serves 2

6 eggs whipped until frothy

2 tablespoons heavy whipping cream

1 ½ cups spinach coarsely chopped

½ cup Parmesan cheese grated

3 tablespoons butter

To Prepare:

In a mixing bowl, combine the eggs and cream and whip until frothy. In a non-stick skillet over medium heat, melt the butter. Add the whipped eggs and cream. Using a wooden spoon stir the bottom of the skillet gently. When the eggs begin to get body, add the spinach and the garlic, stirring them gently into the surface of the co-agulating egg mixture. Try not to push the spinach to the bottom of the skillet to avoid scorching. Reduce the heat to low and cover. Let the frittata steam in the covered skillet to set the eggs, about three to four minutes. Sprinkle the Parmesan cheese over the top and cover once again for about one or two minutes. When the cheese has melted, the frittata is ready to serve. Gently agitate the skillet, holding it at a 45-degree angle and carefully slip the frittata in one piece onto the serving plate.

Ginger Lemon Salmon

Serves 1

1 salmon filet 10-12 ounces

2 tablespoons butter

1 large shallot chopped fine

¾ cup Italian plumb tomatoes de-seeded and diced

1 clove garlic, minced

Juice of one lemon about ¼ cup

2 tablespoons ground ginger, Spice World brand

2 teaspoons fresh parsley chopped

½ cube KNORR® chicken bouillon

To Prepare:

In a non-stick skillet, melt the butter over medium heat. Add the chopped shallot and garlic. Sauté until the shallot becomes translucent, about two minutes. Add the salmon filet and sauté until golden on the bottom before turning the filet. When ready, turn the fish over to golden the other side. After browning both sides of the filet, quickly add the tomatoes, lemon juice, ground ginger, parsley and bouillon to the skillet. Bring the contents of the pan to a simmer. A thin sauce should start to form in three to four minutes. When the sauce is complete and the bouillon has been incorporated, it's ready to serve.

Boneless, skinless chicken breast is good prepared this way too. Always cook chicken until the juices run clear to assure it is fully done.

Chef's Notes

_____

_____

_____

_____

_____

_____

_____

_____

_____

_____

_____

_____

Golden Tilapia Pan Fried with Parmesan Breading

Serves 1

1 large filet golden tilapia

2 tablespoons butter

2 tablespoons olive oil

Ranch dressing or mayonnaise, optional

Breading:

2 tablespoons Parmesan cheese, the pre-grated canned kind is
    best in this case

2 tablespoons Progresso Italian Bread Crumbs

¼ teaspoon Tony Chachere's Original Creole Seasoning

Combine all in a paper plate, mixing well.

To Prepare:

Dredge the filet through the breading mixture, covering well. No pre-coating is necessary. However, if you desire, coat the filet with ranch dressing or mayonnaise, as these will not water down the breading. Heat the oil and butter together in a non-stick skillet over medium heat and pan-fry the fish until golden brown on each side. Do not turn the filet over more than once, to prevent the breading from falling off while cooking. This fish has a most interesting flavor prepared this way. Its flavor is reminiscent of a fried morel mushroom.

Golden Tilapia Stuffed with Deviled Crab

Serves 1

1 large filet golden tilapia

Breading:

¼ cup Progresso Italian Bread Crumbs

2 tablespoons Parmesan

¼ teaspoon Tony Chachere's Original Creole Seasoning

Deviled Crab Stuffing:

6 ounces fancy white crab meat, canned is fine

1 roasted red bell pepper, diced (if canned use ⅛ cup)

1 green onion chopped

1 ½ teaspoons fresh ground extra hot horseradish, Woeber's
    brand

⅛ teaspoon Tony Chachere's Original Creole Seasoning

1 egg white, yellow reserved

To Prepare:

Carefully, with a sharp filet knife, cut a pocket into the thickest part of the filet, slowly working the knife out to the outer edge of the filet without cutting through. Gently stuff the filet with the deviled crab mixture. Once stuffed, beat the reserve egg yolk and brush the stuffed fish and any exposed stuffing with egg yolk. Roll the stuffed filet in the bread crumb mixture, and fry on medium heat in ¼ cup olive oil and two tablespoons of butter for about six minutes on each side, or until all juices from the center run clear.

This dish is a little tedious, due to cutting the pockets, but well worth the effort. You can prepare the fish a day ahead and bread it just before frying. This a great choice for a show-stopping dinner party dish; just multiply the ingredients accordingly.

Chef's Notes

Grilled Caesar Chicken

Serves 6

6 boneless skinless chicken breasts

1 cup Caesar salad dressing

To Prepare:

Coat the chicken breasts with Caesar dressing and grill over medium flame on the grill. Baste the breasts with more dressing with each turn until done. This is much like using barbecue sauce. For extra zing, marinade the chicken in Italian vinaigrette dressing for two or three hours before grilling.

This recipe is also great with butterflied pork chops as a substitution.

Grilled Lemon Thyme Salmon with Green Olive Pesto

Serves 2

1 salmon filet, 1 ½ pounds

In a sealable bag, marinade the salmon filet for 30 minutes prior to grilling. Marinade in ¼ cup lemon juice, two tablespoons olive oil, four large cloves garlic minced, one teaspoon freshly ground black pepper, one tablespoon fresh thyme leaves, lightly chopped. If fresh thyme is not available, dried will do. Reserve this marinade for basting the fish.

Green Olive Pesto:

12 large pimento stuffed Spanish green olives chopped very finely

2 large cloves garlic, minced

2 tablespoons tomato juice

4 tablespoons butter softened

¼ teaspoon freshly ground black pepper

Dash of cayenne pepper

Combine all ingredients in a small bowl until well mixed. The pesto will have a consistency of chunky peanut butter.

To Prepare:

Grill the salmon using the marinade from the sealable bag to baste the fish while grilling. Salmon is best served barely done or a little under done, and cooking time varies with the thickness of the filet. When the salmon is done, dollop a spoon full of the Green Olive Pesto over the top of the hot filet and serve.

Chicken breast is also very good prepared this way, without any substitutions to the recipe except the chicken.

Chef's Notes

Grilled Shark with Ginger Wasabi Pesto

Serves 4

4 shark steaks, 10-12 ounces each
Tony Chachere's Original Creole Seasoning

Marinade:
Juice of one lime
1 tablespoon olive oil
½ teaspoon soy sauce
1 clove garlic, minced

Ginger Wasabi Pesto:
1 tablespoon fresh ground ginger, Spice World brand
2 tablespoons butter softened
½ teaspoon wasabi paste
1 clove garlic, minced
Pinch of cayenne pepper

To Prepare:
Place the shark steaks in a sealable bag. Pour the marinade into the bag, force out as much air as possible, and seal the bag. Marinade the shark steaks in the refrigerator for four hours or overnight. When you are ready to grill the shark steaks, dust them with Tony Chachere's Seasoning to taste. Grill them over medium heat for about four to five minutes on each side. Wait until you are grilling the shark steaks before preparing the pesto, so it doesn't get a chance to set up. To prepare the pesto, combine the ginger, garlic, butter and wasabi with the softened butter in a small bowl stirring until smooth. When the shark is done, plate the steaks and dollop the Ginger Wasabi Pesto over the top and serve. This is a great main dish!

* Thick cut pork chops are good like this too. Simply exchange lime juice for lemon juice and add one tablespoon of teriyaki sauce to the marinade. Delicious!

Chef's Notes

Grilled Shark with Lemon Basil Pesto

Serves 4

4 shark steaks, 10-12 ounces each

Lemon Basil Pesto:

1 cup packed lemon basil leaves

2 cloves garlic

⅛ cup toasted pine nuts

⅓ cup extra virgin olive oil

4 tablespoons butter, softened

¼ cup grated Parmesan cheese

To Prepare:

In a food processor or blender, combine olive oil, garlic, lemon basil and pine nuts. The mixture will liquefy in about 90 seconds. Fold Parmesan cheese and butter into the mixture. Stir together until completely combined, and set aside. Keep the pesto at room temperature until serving. Season the shark with lemon pepper and grill until done, about five minutes. Plate the shark when done, place a generous dollop of the pesto on top of the fish. It will melt over the hot grilled fish. Delightful!

Any remaining pesto can be conserved in the freezer in a covered container for months.

* Try this recipe with boneless skinless chicken breast or pork loin medallions instead of shark. Both go well with the seasonings and pesto.

Chef's Notes

Grilled Swordfish with Ginger Lime Pesto

Serves 4

4 swordfish filets, 10-12 ounces each

Tony Chachere's Original Creole Seasoning

Marinade:

1/2 cup lime juice

1 tablespoon fresh ground ginger, Spice World brand

1/4 teaspoon soy sauce

1/8 teaspoon sesame oil, China Bowl brand

1 clove garlic, minced

1/8 teaspoon cayenne pepper

Ginger Lime Pesto:

2 tablespoons butter

1 tablespoon fresh ground ginger, Spice World brand

2 teaspoons lime juice

1 clove garlic, minced

Dash cayenne pepper

To Prepare:

In a sealable bag, combine all of the ingredients for the marinade. Place the swordfish filets in the bag. Remove as much air from the bag as possible and seal it. Marinade the swordfish in the refrigerator for 30 to 40 minutes. Prepare the Ginger Lime Pesto by combining the softened butter, ground ginger, minced garlic and dash of cayenne pepper in a small microwave-safe bowl. Mix well until smooth. Microwave on high for 20 seconds, just long enough to make the pesto a little soupy. Add lime juice, stirring constantly, so the butter and the juice won't separate. Set the pesto aside while you grill the swordfish. Remove the swordfish from the marinade and grill until cooked through, about five to six minutes per side. To serve, plate the filets and dollop the Ginger Lime Pesto over the top of the grilled filets. Really Good!!!

Chef's Notes

Herbed Chevre Stuffed Salmon

Serves 1 to 2

1 salmon filet, thick cut, about 10-12 ounces

2 ounces chevre cheese

1 teaspoon lemon basil, finely chopped

½ teaspoon freshly ground black pepper

½ teaspoon lemon pepper

1 teaspoon olive oil

1 tablespoon butter

¼ cup dry vermouth

¼ cup lemon juice

To Prepare:

Begin by removing the skin from the salmon filet. Make an incision in the center of the filet that runs the length of the fish. Next flex the incision open so you can see where the incision ends at its depth and cut a pocket back out to the sides of the filet on each side. If you have successfully "surgerized" the filet, it will look like a square piece of pita bread where the bread opens in the middle with pockets on both sides. Now you're ready to make the stuffing. In a small bowl combine the chevre, lemon basil, black and lemon pepper and one tablespoon of olive oil. Stir until smooth. Stuff the pockets of the filet with the cheese stuffing, mounding it out at the incision. In an oven-safe skillet over medium heat, melt the butter. Put the stuffed filet, with stuffing side up, in the pan. Pan-fry until the bottom gets a little golden, about four or five minutes. Add the wine and lemon juice to the skillet and cover allowing the filet to steam for about four to five more minutes. Remove the skillet from the stovetop, and place it beneath a broiler to lightly brown the top of the filet and some of the exposed stuffing. Let the salmon rest for a few minutes before serving. This dish is well worth the effort!

Chef's Notes

Jewels of the Sea in Nectarine Demi Glace

Serves 2

1 pound giant sea scallops

3 tablespoons butter

2 cloves garlic, minced

1 bouquet of fresh herbes de Provence

2 nectarines, halved, pitted and sliced $\frac{1}{8}$ inch thick

To Prepare:

In a non-stick skillet over medium-high heat, melt the butter. Add the minced garlic and herbes de Provence. When the herbs and garlic perfume the air, add the scallops. Sear the scallops on each side until lightly golden, about three or four minutes per side. Remove the scallops from the skillet and place the on the serving plate. Remove the herbs from the skillet and discard them. Return the skillet to the stove and over medium-high heat. Quickly sauté the sliced nectarines in the pan drippings for about two minutes. Place the sautéed nectarines around the scallops. Drizzle the Demi Glace over the top of the scallops and nectarines, and serve.

Demi Glace:

1 bottle peach flavored Chardonnay wine

1 clove garlic, crushed

1 cube KNORR® fish bouillon

3 sprigs fresh marjoram and 1 fresh sprig each of thyme,
      lavender and rosemary

To prepare the Demi Glace, combine all ingredients in a saucepan, bring to a rolling boil, reduce the heat to medium-high, and vigorously simmer until the liquids are reduced to a thick syrup, about 35 to 40 minutes. Remove the saucepan from the heat. Pour the syrup through a fine sieve and set aside.

* Herbes de Provence are a common combination of herbs used quite extensively in southern French cooking. If you can't find it already made up, combine in equal parts: thyme, rosemary, marjoram and lavendar. Often oregano and basil are also added, but I would not suggest it for this recipe.

Chef's Notes

Just Peachy Pork Roast

Serves 4

1 pork loin roast, about 4-5 pounds

4 tablespoons butter

2 cloves garlic, minced, divided

2 sprigs fresh thyme

3 leaves fresh sage

1 cup white wine, chablis or Riesling

1 can peach nectar, 11.3 ounces, Del Valle Nectars brand

1 cube KNORR® chicken bouillon

4 slices thick cut bacon

3 fresh peaches, pitted, peeled and sliced into wedges

Fresh ground black pepper to taste

To Prepare:

In a heavy Dutch oven over medium-high heat, melt the butter. Add the pork loin roast and one clove of minced garlic, searing the roast on all sides until golden. Add the thyme, sage, white wine, peach nectar, the second clove of minced garlic, and chicken bouillon. Bring the liquids to a boil and remove from the heat. Sprinkle the top of the loin roast with fresh ground black pepper, cover, and bake in a 350-degree oven for 30 minutes. Remove roast from the oven, remove the lid, and place the peach wedges overlapping in a row down the length of the roast. Criss-cross the bacon strips gently over the top of the row of peach wedges, lattice style. Return the roast to the oven, uncovered, for another 30 minutes. When done, place the roast on a serving platter and strain the pan drippings over the roast before serving.

If you want a gravy-like sauce, add one cup of heavy whipping cream to the drippings, bring to a boil, and reduce to a sauce, whisking constantly until desired thickness is reached.

To make a Beurre au Peche sauce, bring the strained drippings to a boil. Add one stick of butter, one tablespoon at a time, whisking constantly until all of the butter is combined. Then pour the sauce over the roast before serving.

Chef's Notes

Limey's Fried Codfish

Serves 2 to 4

1 ½ to 2 pounds cod loins, cut into 4 inch portions

Flour for dredging

Marinade:

1 cup lime juice

In a large sealable bag, combine the cod portions and lime juice. Close the sealable bag almost all the way, leaving a small opening, and push all of the air out of the bag before closing. Refrigerate for three to four hours.

Batter:

Combine all ingredients until smooth.

1 cup all purpose flour

³⁄₄ can of beer, dark beer is best

1 egg

2 teaspoons Tony Chachere's Original Creole Seasoning

To Prepare:

Drain the lime juice off the fish. Dredge the fish lightly in flour, then dip the fish in the batter and deep fry at 350-degrees until golden. Drain oil off well, using paper towel. Really tasty!

Mahi Mahi Poached in Mead with Golden Raisins

Serves 1

1 filet mahi mahi, 10-12 ounces

2 tablespoons sweet unsalted butter

2 shallots, finely chopped

⅛ cup golden raisins

1 ½ cups of mead, a wine made from honey

1 clove garlic, minced

½ cube KNORR® fish bouillon

To Prepare:

In a non-stick skillet over medium heat, melt the butter, add shallots and sauté for one minute. Add mahi mahi and sauté until lightly golden on each side, about four minutes per side. Increase the heat to medium-high, and add minced garlic, mead and bouillon. The sauce will come to a boil quickly. When the liquids are reduced by half, add the raisins and remove from heat. Plate the fish and pour the sauce and raisins over the top. Delicious!

* Alternatives include both pork loin medallions and chicken breast. For these alternatives, use chicken bouillon instead of fish.

Chef's Notes

Mahi Mahi in Royal Crab Sauce Velouté

Serves 1

1 mahi mahi filet, 10-12 ounces

½ of a snow crab, in shell

½ cup brandy

2 cloves garlic, minced and divided

2 pinches cayenne pepper

3 pinches ground white pepper

½ cube KNORR® fish bouillon

1 cup heavy cream

2 tablespoons brie cheese, crust removed

1 tablespoon butter

To Prepare:

Combine in a saucepan: crab in shell, cayenne pepper, white pepper, one clove minced garlic, fish bouillon and brandy. Simmer on medium-high heat until liquids reduce by ⅔. Remove pan from heat, remove crab from pan and place on a plate to cool. Reserve the reduced liquids in the saucepan. Extract the crab from shells, reserving the meat and any extra drippings discard shells. Bring the remaining liquids in the saucepan to a low simmer, add heavy cream and brie to the simmering liquids. Stir the sauce constantly, until smooth. When smooth, reduce heat to warm.

In a non-stick skillet, melt one tablespoon of butter and add one clove minced garlic, keeping heat on a medium setting. Add mahi mahi; sauté on each side slowly until lightly golden. Careful, try not to scorch the butter. When lightly golden, pour the cream sauce into the skillet, add crabmeat and let simmer until done, about three minutes. Delicious!!!

Chef's Notes

Mongolian Monk Fish

Serves 2

1 filet of monk fish, 10-12 ounces, membrane removed, and sliced into ¼ inch thick medallions

2 cloves garlic, minced

6 scallions, whites chopped, greens cut into 1 inch long pieces

2 tablespoons olive oil

1 medium sweet onion cut into wedges

Sauce:

2 tablespoons soy sauce

2 tablespoons honey

1 tablespoon dry vermouth

1 tablespoon Szechwan sauce, KA-ME brand

To Prepare:

To prepare the sauce, combine ingredients in a small bowl and set aside.

In a non-stick skillet, heat the olive oil on high heat and add the onion wedges. Stir-fry until lightly golden on the edges, about two minutes. Add the fish, white of scallion and garlic. Stir-fry until the fish turns opaque, about two minutes. Add the sauce and let it thicken, about two minutes.

Add the greens of the scallion and stir-fry for one minute or until the greens turn bright green. Serve on top of mung bean sprouts. Yummy!!!

* Try substituting boneless skinless chicken breast or pork loin sliced into ¼ inch medallions for another tasty alternative.

Pan Seared Salmon with Black Bean Sauce

Serves 1

1 filet of salmon, 10-12 ounces

1 tablespoon butter

1 tablespoon fresh ground ginger, Spice World brand

1 heaping tablespoon black bean sauce, KA-ME brand

½ cube KNORR® chicken bouillon

Scant ½ cup white zinfandel wine

1 clove garlic, minced .

To Prepare:

Over medium-high heat, melt the butter in a non-stick skillet. Sear the salmon until lightly golden on each side, about three minutes per side. Add the remaining ingredients, gently stirring the sauce around the fish. Turn the filet gently as the sauce reduces to a syrup-like consistency, about three minutes. Place the filet on the serving plate and pour the sauce over the top of the filet to serve.

* Pork medallions are good like this too; the recipe requires no other substitution other than the choice of meat.

Chef's Notes

Parmesan Crusted Haddock

Serves 4 to 6

2 pounds haddock filets cut into 3 inch long pieces

½ cup grated Parmesan cheese, canned is best in this case

½ cup Progresso Italian Bread Crumbs

1 teaspoon basil flakes

1 teaspoon oregano flakes

1 teaspoon garlic powder

¼ teaspoon freshly ground black pepper

⅛ teaspoon cayenne pepper, optional

Juice of one lemon

2 eggs

¼ cup heavy whipping cream

1 cup olive oil, for frying

To Prepare:

On a paper plate, combine Parmesan cheese, bread crumbs, basil, oregano, garlic powder, black pepper and cayenne. Mix well until the breading is homogenous. In a bowl, lightly beat the eggs and cream together to make an egg wash. Dip each piece of fish in the egg wash, then dredge through the prepared breading. Heat the olive oil over medium heat in a non-stick skillet, add the fish and fry until golden brown on all sides. Drain the fried fish when done onto paper toweling before plating onto a serving tray. Drizzle lemon juice over the top and garnish with parsley sprigs before serving. Fantastic!

Try this breading with boneless skinless chicken breast for a great new and different way to fry chicken. For a little twist, try using fresh squeezed orange juice drizzled over the top, and serve with orange slices on the platter, molto Italiano!

Chef's Notes

Poached Filet of Sole Stuffed with Deviled Shrimp

Serves 4

4 filets of sole

White wine for poaching, chablis works well

Deviled shrimp:

1 cup shrimp coarsely chopped, pre-cooked

1 egg white lightly beaten with one tablespoon white wine

2 scallions chopped coarsely (white and greens)

2 tablespoons roasted red bell peppers, chopped coarsely,
     Frieda's brand is best

1 tablespoon ground horseradish, Woeber's brand

2 pinches cayenne pepper

⅓ teaspoon Tony Chachere's Original Creole Seasoning

2 tablespoons bread crumbs made from pulverized
     Caesar croutons

To Prepare:

Gently combine all ingredients for the deviled shrimp. Place sole filets flat on a cutting board. Gently pat a layer of the deviled shrimp on top of each filet about ¼ inch thick. Roll the filet into a roll or pinwheel, using four squares of aluminum foil about eight inches square. Place one teaspoon of butter in the center. Place the fish roll on end atop the butter and wrap the foil around the sides of the fish to hold the roll together, leaving the top of the roll exposed. Spoon on the remaining shrimp mixture, mounding evenly on the top of each roll, then seal the foil up to encapsulate the roll. Place the rolls. mounded end up, in a shallow baking dish and pour white wine in the bottom of the dish, about ¼ inch deep. Pre-heat the oven to 375 degrees and poach fish rolls for about 30 minutes. Remove the baking dish from the oven and open the foil, exposing the top of each roll. Lightly sprinkle bread crumbs over the top of each roll and return the dish to the oven for another 15 minutes or until golden on top. Carefully remove the fish rolls from the foil, reserving any drippings in the foil as well as the remaining wine in the dish used for poaching. Place on a serving plate and spoon Sauce Velouté (see next page) over the top before serving.

Sauce Velouté:

While removing foil from fish rolls, carefully drain off excess liquids at bottom of the roll into the wine used for poaching. Pour the contents of the baking dish through a sieve into a saucepan. Add ½ cube of KNORR® fish or shrimp bouillon, heat over high heat, and reduce the liquids until thick. Add ⅔ cup heavy whipping cream and bring to a brisk simmer whisking constantly. Continue to reduce the cream until the sauce thickens, about five minutes. When done, spoon the sauce over the fish rolls and serve.

I like to serve this with Finocchio alla Campagnola, see page 192. The flavors complement each other and make a great presentation. A great dish to "wow" guests!

Chef's Notes

_____

_____

_____

_____

_____

_____

_____

_____

_____

_____

_____

_____

Poached Sea Bass

Serves 2

2 portions of sea bass, 10-12 ounces each

2 tablespoons butter

2 shallots, diced finely

1 clove garlic, minced

½ cup mead, a wine made from honey

½ cube KNORR® fish bouillon

2 Italian plumb tomatoes, de-seeded and diced fine

1 tablespoon fresh Italian parsley, chopped

1 tablespoon fresh chives, chopped

To Prepare:

In a non-stick skillet, melt the butter. Add shallots and garlic, sauté for one minute over medium heat. Add the fish; cook on both sides for three minutes. Increase the heat to high. Add the mead and bouillon. Cover and let the fish poach for about three minutes. Remove the lid; add diced tomatoes, parsley and chives. Simmer, uncovered, for about two minutes or until the tomatoes begin to sauce just a little. Plate the fish and serve with the sauce from the pan ladled over the top.

* Chicken breast makes a nice substitute in this dish. If you want to try this recipe with chicken, substitute chicken bouillon for the fish bouillon and add a dash of cayenne pepper for a little extra kick.

Chef's Notes

Poached Stuffed Orange Roughy

Serves 2

2 filets of orange roughy

1 leek, with good long greens

1 can, 4 ounces, shrimp, washed and drained

1 can, 4 ounces, mushroom caps and pieces, drained

1 small onion, minced

½ cup grated Parmesan cheese, canned is best in this case

⅛ teaspoon cayenne pepper

4 tablespoons dry vermouth

White wine for poaching, chablis works well

To Start:

Begin by carefully separating two good, sturdy leaves from the leek. Blanch them in boiling water for one to two minutes or until pliable remove them from the water, and set aside. Remove the white portion with only the very light green part from the leek and reserve it for the stuffing.

For the stuffing, chop the white part (only) of the leek, shrimp, onion and mushrooms very finely. Transfer to a small mixing bowl and combine with ¼ cup of Parmesan cheese, cayenne pepper and vermouth.

To Prepare:

Pat the filets of orange roughy dry, with paper toweling. Lay them out flat on a cutting board. Using half of the stuffing, spread each filet evenly, about ¼ inch thick, sparing the last 1½ inches at the tail end of the filet. Pat the stuffing down tight like a hamburger patty. Fold the tail end of the fish over the packed stuffing and gently form the filet into a roll. Secure the roll with a piece of kitchen string or a rubber band momentarily, to keep its shape. Take one of the blanched leek fronds, lay it flat on the cutting board. Center the fish roll in the middle of the leek frond and use the frond like a ribbon tying a knot with the free ends around the rolled up fish. Remove the kitchen string or rubber band and set the tied fish roll on end in a glass baking dish. Repeat for the other filets. Crown the rolls with the remaining stuffing, mounding it on the tops. Cover the top of the stuffing with remaining Parmesan cheese. Pour any dry white wine in the bottom of the glass baking dish about ½ inch deep. Cover with aluminum foil, and bake in a pre-heated oven at 350 degrees for 30 minutes. Remove the aluminum foil from the top and return the fish to the oven uncovered for another 15 minutes or until the top is lightly golden.

For a sauce to spoon over the poached fish, pour the remaining drippings in the glass dish through a mesh sieve into a saucepan. Bring the liquids to a boil, add one tablespoon of lemon juice and one cup of heavy whipping cream. Bring back to a boil and add fresh chopped dill weed. Tasty!

Chef's Notes

Poached Stuffed Tilapia with Beurre Limone

Serves 4

4 tilapia filets, cut in half lengthwise and split lengthwise
to create 2 long ribbon filets per filet of tilapia

1 cup white zinfandel wine

Filling:

6 ounces lump crab meat, canned

6 ounces lobster slipper meat, cooked and shredded

12 jumbo shrimp, pre-cooked, tails removed, chopped medium

1 large clove garlic, minced

1 shallot, minced

4 ounces cream cheese, softened

2 tablespoons Parmesan cheese, pre-grated

⅛ teaspoon ground white pepper

Beurre Limone:

One stick of butter

Strained liquids from poaching. See method below.

To Prepare:

Soften the cream cheese in the microwave, using a glass bowl, about one minute. Stir in crabmeat, shrimp, lobster, garlic, shallot, Parmesan cheese and white pepper. Lay ribbons of filets out lengthwise, and spread filling out ¼ inch thick over the length of the ribbon. Form the ribbon into a roll, beginning with the widest end of the ribbon. The resulting roll will look like a rosebud. Fold an eight inch wide piece of aluminum foil in half. Place the rolled tilapia in the center of the foil and fold the foil around the base of the roll making a jacket, about one inch tall, around the roll. Flare the exposed edges of the fish out so the roll looks like an opening rosebud. Place the jacketed rolls in a glass-baking dish just large enough to fit all eight rolls, sparing ½ inch between the rolls and the sides of the glass dish. Pour one cup of white zinfandel in the bottom of the glass-baking dish. Bake, uncovered, in a 450-degree pre-heated oven for 35 to 45 minutes or until the tips of the fish and stuffing are gently golden. When the fish is done remove the rolls from the baking dish. Set them aside on a plate to rest.

Add ½ cup of lemon juice to the remaining liquids in the baking dish. Using a fork or whisk, scrape off any caramelized juices from the sides of the dish and incorporate the caramelized scrapings into the drippings. Strain the liquids using a fine mesh sieve into a saucepan and reduce over high heat stirring constantly until the fluids are reduced to a medium-thick syrup. Remove from the stove and add the room temperature butter to the saucepan, one tablespoon at a time, whisking until the butter is completely melted and a smooth sauce remains. This is the Beurre Limone sauce. Remove the fish from their jackets and plate. Drizzle the sauce over the top of the rolls and decoratively around the plate. Garnish with freshly chopped parsley and serve.

*   You may substitute monkfish for the lobster by boiling the monkfish in water and one tablespoon of crab boil. Drain off the water when done, and shred. Tastes a lot like lobster.*

Chef's Notes

Pollo alla Rosticceria
Roast Chicken Italian Style

Serves 4

1 large roasting chicken

4 cloves garlic, minced

3 fresh sprigs rosemary

2 large sweet onions quartered

1 tablespoon fresh ground black pepper

1 ½ teaspoons reduced sodium salt

¼ cup olive oil

To Prepare:

Remove any contents from the cavity of the bird, and wash well before cooking, inside and out. In a measuring cup, combine the olive oil, minced garlic, black pepper, salt and the leaves from two of the three sprigs of rosemary and set aside. Stuff the cavity of the chicken with the onion quarters and place the third sprig of rosemary in the center of the bird. Rub the herb mixture prepared with olive oil over the skin of the chicken. Stick your finger just under the skin covering the breast of the bird on both sides and make little pockets. Stuff 1½ tablespoons of butter into each pocket under the skin of the breast; this will help keep the breast meat moist. Place the dressed bird on a rack in a covered Dutch oven. If you don't have a rack, use a couple of ribs of celery under the bird instead. Roast the chicken in a pre-heated 375-degree oven covered for 35 minutes. Remove the lid and baste the bird with some of the juices in the bottom of the pan and return it to the oven uncovered for another 25-35 minutes, or until the chicken's skin is golden and the juices run clear. When done, remove the chicken from the oven and let it stand for about 10 minutes before serving.

Chef's Notes

Pork Loin in Shitake Dijon Sauce

Serves 4

2 pounds pork loin cut into ½ inch thick medallions

½ pound shitake mushrooms cut into wedges

3 tablespoons butter

2 cloves garlic, minced

One dash white pepper

½ cup Cognac

1 cube KNORR® chicken bouillon

1 heaping soup spoon Dijon mustard

1 pint heavy whipping cream

To Prepare:

In a heavy skillet over medium-high heat, melt the butter. Add the pork medallions and shitake mushrooms. Sear the medallions until lightly golden on each side, about three to four minutes each side. Add the minced garlic and dash of white pepper and sauté for two minutes to emulsify. Add the Cognac carefully so it doesn't ignite, and add the chicken bouillon so it can dissolve. De-glaze the medallions quickly on both sides. When the bouillon has dissolved, remove the medallions from the pan and set aside. Increase the heat to high and reduce the Cognac until it's thick and bubbly. Quickly whisk the Dijon mustard into the reduced Cognac and add the heavy whipping cream. Constantly stirring, bring the sauce back up to a strong simmer. Add the medallions back to the pan and warm them through in the sauce, about two minutes. This is a wonderfully rich and satisfying main dish. Try serving it with the Savory Beans recipe on page 202.

Chef's Notes

Pork Medallions Scaloppini

Serves 4

2 pounds pork loin cut into ½ inch thick medallions

2 tablespoons butter

2 tablespoons olive oil

2 cloves garlic, minced

⅓ cup dry white wine

Juice of one lemon

½ cup Progresso Italian Bread Crumbs

½ teaspoon white pepper

To Prepare:

Lightly dredge the medallions in the peppered bread crumbs. In a heavy non-stick skillet over medium heat, melt the butter in the olive oil. Add the dredged medallions and gently fry until golden brown on both sides.

Remove the medallions from the pan and set aside. To the drippings in the pan

add the wine and increase the heat to high. Reduce the wine to a thick bubbling consistency. Add the lemon juice, stirring through the reduced wine until sauce forms. Return the medallions back to the sauce in the skillet, coating each side with sauce, and serve.

Portobello Mushrooms Stuffed with Lobster Claws

Serves 2

2 large portobello mushrooms, stems and gills gently scraped out to leave caps behind, stems reserved and chopped for the stuffing later.

2 cloves garlic, minced

4 shallots, diced finely

1 tablespoon fresh chives, chopped finely

1 cup lobster slipper meat, cooked and shredded

2 lobster claws, shells removed gently so the meat remains intact

1 cup shredded Monterey jack cheese

⅛ teaspoon cayenne pepper

2 tablespoons dry vermouth

½ cube KNORR® fish bouillon

To Prepare:

In a mixing bowl, combine chopped stems reserved from the mushroom caps with the lobster slipper meat, garlic, shallots chives, Monterey jack cheese and cayenne pepper. In an oven-safe cup, in the microwave, heat two tablespoons of vermouth with the fish bouillon for 30 seconds. Add the vermouth and bouillon mixture to the stuffing mixture. Stir ingredients together well. Stuff the mushroom caps, using all of the mixture. Place one lobster claw on top of each stuffed mushroom. Choose a glass baking dish just large enough to fit the stuffed mushroom caps. Pour two tablespoons of melted butter and one clove of minced garlic in the bottom of the dish. Place the stuffed mushrooms, stuffing side up, in the dish. Bake at 350 degrees in a pre-heated oven, covered lightly, until the mushrooms are tender and the stuffing is bubbly, about 25-30 minutes. To serve, place each mushroom on a plate and garnish with fresh chopped chives. Incredible!

Chef's Notes

Poulet à la Dijon

Serves 6

6 boneless skinless chicken breasts

2 tablespoons butter

1 clove garlic, minced

³/₄ cup dry white wine

1 cube KNORR® chicken bouillon

2 soup spoons Dijon mustard

1 pint heavy whipping cream

To Prepare:

In a large heavy skillet over high heat, melt the butter. Add the garlic and place the chicken breasts in the skillet searing each side until golden brown. Add the wine and bouillon. Continue cooking on high until the liquids are reduced by ³/₄. Remove the chicken from the skillet and reduce the remaining liquids until thick and bubbly. Quickly add the mustard stirring with a whisk. Reduce the heat to medium and quickly whisk in the cream. Bring the sauce back to a strong simmer and return the chicken to the sauce to heat through, about four minutes. This is a classic dish and it goes great with Cavolfiore al Forno, on page 190.

Red Snapper alla Siciliana

Serves 1

One filet red snapper, 10-12 ounces

1 tablespoon olive oil

1 cup Italian plumb tomatoes, skinned de-seeded and diced

1 small onion, diced finely

2 cloves garlic, minced

1 tablespoon capers

¼ cup dry vermouth

1 teaspoon anchovy paste, Giovanni's Anchovy paste is the best

Black pepper to taste

¼ cup sliced black olives

2 small dried red chili peppers, crushed

To Prepare:

In a non-stick skillet, heat the olive oil over medium-high heat. Sear the red snapper on each side until lightly golden, about three minutes each side. De-glaze the pan with the dry vermouth and add the remaining ingredients. Continue to simmer the ingredients until a light sauce forms from the tomatoes, about two minutes. Plate and serve with the sauce poured over the top. Yummy!

Chef's Notes

_____

_____

_____

_____

_____

_____

_____

_____

_____

_____

_____

_____

Roast Pork Loin Champagnoise

Serves 4 to 6

4 pounds pork loin, fat removed

½ stick butter

4 cloves garlic, minced

2 cubes KNORR® chicken bouillon

¾ of a bottle of dry Champagne, an inexpensive brand is fine

1 quart heavy whipping cream

White pepper to taste

To Prepare:

In a large heavy Dutch oven, melt the butter on high heat. Add the pork loin and sear it on all sides until golden brown. Add the minced garlic and Champagne. Reduce the heat to medium and add the bouillon and fresh ground white pepper to taste, no more that four to five turns. Cover and continue to simmer on medium for about one hour. Remove the pork roast from the Dutch oven and set aside. Pour the remaining liquids through a strainer to clarify the sauce and wipe out the inside of the Dutch oven before returning the strained liquids to the pan. Turn the heat up to high bring the liquids to a boil and reduce them until reduced to a thick bubbly consistency. Add the cream and stir with a whisk thoroughly. Return the roast to the sauce and warm it through, about 10-15 minutes. Slice the loin into medallions and pour the sauce over the meat before serving. This dish is an elegant choice for holidays or for a nice dinner party.

Ruby Trout in Dilled Tomato Cream Sauce

Serves 1

1 large filet ruby trout, a.k.a. rainbow trout

1 tablespoon butter

½ cup tomato juice

½ cube KNORR® chicken or fish bouillon

2 ounces brie cheese, crust removed

½ teaspoon dill weed, chopped finely; fresh is best,
        but dried will do

To Prepare:

In a non-stick skillet over medium-high heat, melt the butter, add the trout filet, and sauté until cooked on one side, about two minutes. Turn the filet over and add the tomato juice, bouillon and brie gently, stir in the bouillon and cheese to dissolve them in the tomato juice. When the sauce is homogenous, about three minutes, add the dill weed and simmer for about another minute to fully invest the flavor of the dill into the sauce. To serve, plate the fish onto a dish with raised sides, pour the sauce over the filet, and garnish with a fresh sprig of dill weed. Yum!

This dish can very easily be changed to suit chicken lovers too. Simply use boneless skinless chicken breasts in place of trout and use chicken bouillon instead of fish. Cooking times will also be altered. You will need to cook the chicken on both sides for about six minutes or until golden on each side before you begin making the sauce. After the chicken is browned, proceed with the sauce as described above. This recipe is designed for one serving, so remember to multiply accordingly if you are serving more people.

Chef's Notes

Salmon à la Dijon

Serves 1

1 salmon filet 10-12 ounces, skin removed

2 tablespoons butter, divided

2 cloves garlic, divided and minced

½ cup white zinfandel wine

½ cube KNORR® fish bouillon

1 soup spoon Dijon mustard

½ cup heavy whipping cream

Fresh ground pepper, 2-3 turns or to taste

1 large portobello mushroom sliced thick (like sliced bread)

1 tablespoon olive oil

To Prepare:

In a non-stick skillet over medium-high heat, melt one tablespoon of butter and one tablespoon of olive oil together. Add one clove of minced garlic and large sliced portabella mushroom to the pan. Sauté until golden on each side. Season with fresh ground pepper to taste. Remove the mushroom slices when done and place them on a serving plate. Remove any garlic pieces or residue from the skillet and return it to the stove over medium-high heat. Add one tablespoon of butter, one clove of garlic and fresh ground pepper to the skillet. Place the salmon in the skillet and sear each side until lightly golden on each side, about two minutes per side. Add wine and fish bouillon, and cook the salmon for one minute on each side. Remove the filet from the pan, placing it on top of the mushroom slices. Continue cooking the sauce until reduced to a thick bubbly consistency. Add the Dijon mustard, whisking constantly. Quickly add the cream, whisking. When the sauce has formed and all is well combined, return the fish to the sauce. Reduce the heat to medium and simmer gently for two minutes on each side. When done, place the fish on the mushroom slices and pour the sauce over the fish before serving. This dish is both elegant and delicious.

Chef's Notes

Salmon au Gratin

Serves 1

1 filet of salmon, about 10-12 ounces, skin removed

8-10 large shrimp, peeled, de-veined and tails removed

2 tablespoons butter

2 shallots finely chopped, or ½ small sweet onion may be substituted if shallots aren't available

1 clove garlic, minced

½ cube KNORR® chicken bouillon or fish bouillon

¼ cup Champagne or white wine

⅓ cup heavy whipping cream

4 ounces brie crust removed

2 tablespoons bread crumbs (optional)

Dash cayenne pepper

Pinch of nutmeg

To Prepare:

In a non-stick pan over medium-high heat, melt the butter. Add shallots and sauté for 30 seconds. Add the fish, reduce the heat to medium, and pan-fry on each side until lightly golden, about four minutes. Add the Champagne, chicken bouillon and minced garlic. Increase the heat to medium-high and simmer until the bouillon is dissolved. Remove the fish from the pan and set aside in a small baking dish. Increase the heat to high, and continue simmering the sauce until reduced by half, about four minutes. Add the cheese and reduce heat to medium, stirring constantly until melted. Add the cream slowly, stirring constantly. Add the shrimp bring to a slow boil. Pour the shrimp and sauce over the fish in the baking dish. The sauce should just cover the filet so it is not exposed. Sprinkle cayenne pepper and nutmeg over the top lightly. If you use the bread crumbs, sprinkle them over the top now. Broil for three minutes or until top of sauce bubbles and is lightly golden. This is a very satisfying and soul-warming dish in cold weather.

Chef's Notes

Salmon in Champagne Shitake Mushroom Sauce

Serves 1

1 salmon filet, 10-12 ounces

1 tablespoon butter

⅓ cup Champagne

2 walnut sized pieces of brie, crust removed

½ cube KNORR® fish bouillon

3-4 shitake mushrooms, stems removed, with cap cut like a pie
into about 6 pieces each

⅓ cup heavy whipping cream

To Prepare:

In a non-stick skillet over high heat, melt the butter. Add shitake mushrooms sauté for about four minutes, stirring constantly. Move mushrooms over to one side of the pan, add the salmon and sear on both sides until lightly golden about two minutes. Add Champagne and fish bouillon, and remove fish from pan while you reduce the liquids until thick and bubbly. Add the cream and brie, stirring constantly until the cheese has melted. Return the salmon to the sauce to warm through for about two minutes. Serve with the sauce poured over the top. This is a great entrée with a flavor that is incredible. I've heard people who say they don't like salmon absolutely love this!

Salmon with Blackberry Merlot Demi Glace

Serves 2

2 salmon filets, 10-12 ounces each, thick cut

2 tablespoons sweet unsalted butter

2 shallots, chopped finely

½ teaspoon Tony Chachere's Original Creole Seasoning, divided

Demi Glace:

1 bottle blackberry flavored merlot wine

1 cube KNORR® chicken bouillon

2 cloves garlic, minced

⅛ teaspoon freshly ground black peppercorns

1 large sprig of fresh rosemary

To Prepare:

In a large non-stick saucepan, combine all of the ingredients for the Demi Glace. Bring to a boil on high heat. When liquids begin to boil vigorously, reduce the heat to medium-high to prevent boil over or scorching. Continue boiling until the liquids are reduced by 80% to 90% and the remaining residue is like thin syrup, about 35 to 40 minutes. Set aside; this may be made ahead and reserved in the fridge for quite a while. In a large non-stick skillet, melt the butter over medium heat. Add half of the Tony's Tony Chachere's Seasoning and the shallots. When the shallots become transparent, add the salmon filets. Sauté the filets until lightly golden on one side. Before turning, dust the filets with the remaining seasoning, turn over, and sauté until golden on second side. When the fish is done, add the Demi Glace to the pan, to warm before drizzling over the salmon. Garnish with a fresh sprig of rosemary. WOW!

Filet mignon, thick center cut pork chops or lamb loin are all great substitutes which require no other changes in this recipe.

Chef's Notes

_____

_____

_____

_____

_____

_____

_____

_____

_____

_____

Scampi

Serves 1 to 2

12-14 extra large tiger prawns, shelled and de-veined

3 tablespoons sweet unsalted butter

3-4 large cloves garlic, minced

$\frac{1}{8}$ teaspoon cayenne pepper

Juice of one lemon

$\frac{1}{2}$ cup dry vermouth or Chardonnay

$\frac{1}{2}$ cube KNORR® fish bouillon

1 tablespoon fresh chives chopped medium fine

To Prepare:

In a non-stick skillet, heat the butter over medium-high heat. When the butter begins to bubble add the prawns, cayenne and garlic, and sauté for about two minutes on each side. Add wine, lemon juice, bouillon and half the chives.

Cook for one minute, then remove prawns from the pan, arranging them on a warmed plate for serving. Continue cooking the liquids in the skillet until they reduce to a thickened sauce. Add the other half of the chives. Stir them through the sauce to warm them, then pour the sauce over the top of the plated prawns. Garnish with a few chive sprigs. Great as an appetizer too!

Seared Peppercorn Salmon with Bourbon Honey Glaze

Serves 1

1 filet of salmon, 10-12 ounces

1 tablespoon butter

Freshly milled or crushed black peppercorns

Tony Chachere's Original Creole Seasoning

$\frac{1}{3}$ cup Bourbon whiskey

1 tablespoon honey

To Prepare:

Combine the Bourbon and honey in a measuring cup, stirring well until honey is dissolved. Melt one tablespoon of butter in a non-stick pan over low heat. Mill peppercorns over the bottom of the pan generously. Sprinkle Tony Chachere's Original Creole Seasoning over the crushed peppercorns, about one teaspoon. Lay the salmon filet over the pepper and seasoning, and increase heat to medium, searing the salmon, about four minutes, depending on thickness. Sear until half done before turning the filet over. While searing the first side, coat the other side with black peppercorns and Tony Chachere's Seasoning. Sear the other side for four to five minutes. When the fish is ready it will begin to split open a little. Add half of the whiskey and honey mixture to the pan, agitating the skillet gently to evenly de-glaze the fish. When liquids reduce to a bubbly residue (about $\frac{1}{4}$ remaining) turn the fish over and de-glaze the other side with the remaining bourbon and honey mixture. When the liquids are reduced to a bubbly residue place the fish on a plate and pour the remaining liquids over the top of the filet before serving. Delicious!!!

* Beef filets and pork loin medallions are both great substitutes. Pork loin filets must be cooked through, but the beef may be cooked as desired. Undercook a little; the de-glazing will cook them more quickly. Pork loin and beef filets: follow the same recipe except add one tablespoon of Dijon mustard to the bourbon and honey mixture.*

Chef's Notes

Seared Tuna in Sweet Hot Sauce

Serves 1

1 filet of tuna, 10-12 ounces

2 cloves garlic, minced, divided

1 tablespoon sesame oil, China Bowl brand

1 teaspoon fresh black pepper, divided

Sauce:

1 tablespoon soy sauce

1 teaspoon ground ginger, Spice World brand

2 teaspoons honey

1 teaspoon rice wine vinegar

1/8 teaspoon cayenne pepper

To Prepare:

Heat the oil in a non-stick pan on high, add half of the garlic and fresh ground black pepper. Add the tuna and sear, agitating frequently to prevent scorching. While searing the first side, spread the remaining garlic and pepper on the uncooked side.

Turn the fish over to sear the other side. Cook each side for three to four minutes, then add half of the sauce. Allow the sauce to caramelize, becoming thick and bubbly, then turn the filet over and add the remaining sauce. When the sauce gets thick and bubbly again, transfer the fish to a serving plate and pour the caramelized sauce in the pan over the fish.

For extra zing add a dollop of Wasabi Pesto on top before serving. Recipe for pesto is on page 116.

* Chicken may be substituted for tuna without other changes to the ingredients. Technique, however, is a little different. Begin by searing the chicken on medium heat. You want the meat cooked thoroughly; otherwise finish as above.

Chef's Notes

Sea Scallops with Balsamic Rosemary Berry Reduction

Serves 2

16 large sea scallops

4 slices of thick sliced bacon cut into ¼ inch ribbons

2 cloves garlic, minced

1 tablespoon fresh chives, finely chopped

Reduction:

½ cube of KNORR® chicken bouillon

½ cup of good quality balsamic vinegar

¼ cup fresh raspberry pulp, see method

1 clove garlic, minced

2 sprigs fresh rosemary or 2 teaspoons dried rosemary leaves

1 ½ cups raspberry flavored zinfandel wine

To Prepare:

Begin by preparing the reduction. Combine all ingredients in a saucepan and bring to a boil. Reduce to a strong simmer and continue to cook until the sauce becomes thick and syrupy. Strain reduction through a fine mesh sieve and set aside.

Cook the bacon until browned but not crispy. Remove the bacon from the skillet, and set aside on a paper towel to drain off excess oils. Add the garlic and scallops to the bacon drippings. Cook over a medium-high heat until the scallops are done; they should be slightly browned, about four to five minutes. Add the chives and bacon. Sauté for one minute. Transfer contents to a hot serving plate. Add the reduction to the skillet in which the scallops were prepared to quickly re-heat the reduction. Drizzle the reduction over and around the plated scallops. Garnish with fresh raspberries and rosemary sprigs. Incredibly explosive taste! "Oh My God Good!" I recommend serving this with my recipe for Smoked Turkey and Wild Rice Salad on page 74. Mound the salad in the center of the plate, scatter the scallops and fresh raspberries over the mound of salad, and drizzle the reduction over the top.

Chef's Notes

Sesame Tuna with Ginger Balsamic Reduction

Serves 1

1 sushi grade tuna steak, about 10-12 ounces and
     1½ inches thick

1 egg white

1 tablespoon rice wine vinegar

6 tablespoons sesame seeds divided into thirds

1 tablespoon grapeseed oil

Reduction:

¼ cup good quality balsamic vinegar

1 clove garlic, minced

1 teaspoon sliced pickled ginger

1 pinch cayenne pepper

To Prepare:

Begin with the reduction. Combine the ingredients in a saucepan. Bring to a boil continue cooking until thick and syrupy, about 10 - 15 minutes. Strain through a fine sieve when done and set aside.

To prepare the tuna: In a dry non-stick skillet, toast ⅓ of the sesame seeds to a medium brown color, five to six minutes, stirring constantly so they color up evenly and don't scorch. When done, transfer to a paper plate. Toast the next third of the sesame seeds lightly until just golden, three to four minutes. Transfer these and the last third of the sesame seeds to the paper plate with the first third of darker toasted seeds. Mix the seeds around, so the mixture looks like tri-colored confetti, and set aside. Whisk together the egg white and rice vinegar until frothy. Brush the fish on top and bottom with the egg wash, keeping the sides of the steak clean. Sprinkle the sesame seeds over the brushed surface of the fish to create a breading on top and bottom but not the sides. Reason? So you can see how well done the fish is becoming. Next, heat the grapeseed oil in a skillet on medium-high heat. Sear the fish on both sides, rare takes about two minutes on each side. To serve, pool the reduction on the serving plate. Place fish on the pooled reduction and garnish with wasabi and pickled ginger slices. For you sushi lovers, this dish is perfect.

Chef's Notes

Shrimp with Sugar Snap Peas and Asparagus

Serves 2

³/₄ pound jumbo pre-cooked shrimp, tails removed

1 pound sugar snap peas

1 pound asparagus, cut into 1½ inch pieces

½ medium sweet onion, wedged into thirds

2 scallions, with whites·chopped greens cut into 1 inch pieces

½ cup English walnut halves

2 teaspoons Hot Oil, China Bowl brand

Sauce:

2 cloves garlic, minced

2 tablespoons ground ginger, Spice World brand

2 tablespoons Black Bean Sauce, KA-ME brand

1 to 2 teaspoons Szechwan Sauce, KA-ME brand

1 teaspoon KNORR® liquid chicken bouillon

To Prepare:

In a non-stick skillet, heat China Bowl Hot Oil over high heat setting. Add the sweet onion and stir-fry for about two minutes to gently brown. Add frozen sugar snap peas and asparagus, continuing to stir-fry until the vegetables are bright green and tender yet crisp, about three minutes. Quickly add the sauce and shrimp. When the sauce coats the ingredients and has thickened, add walnuts and scallions. Combine well, about one minute, and transfer to serving plate. This dish is relatively quick to prepare and is incredibly tasty.

Chicken is easily substituted for the shrimp in this recipe. Simply cut two boneless skinless chicken breasts into ⅛ inch thick strips on the bias and add them into the pan with the sweet onion. Follow the rest of the recipe just as stated for the rest.

Chef's Notes

Suprême de Volaille avec Sauce D'Abricots Velouté
Chicken Breast in Apricot Cream Sauce

Serves 4

4 boneless, skinless chicken breasts

2 tablespoons butter

2 cloves garlic, minced

1 sprig fresh rosemary

2 nectarines, pitted and sliced into ⅛ inch thick wedges

¼ cup citrus or peach flavored vodka

1 can, 11.3 ounces, apricot nectar, Del Valle Nectars brand

1 cup heavy whipping cream

1 cube KNORR® chicken bouillon

To Prepare:

In a heavy non-stick skillet, melt the butter over medium to medium-high heat. Add the chicken breast and sauté until golden on both sides. Add the garlic, rosemary and vodka, de-glazing the chicken on both sides. Add the apricot nectar, chicken bouillon and the heavy whipping cream. Bring the sauce to a boil and reduce the heat to a medium simmer. At this point the chicken should be nearly done. Remove the breasts from the sauce, setting them aside on a serving plate with sides. Continue to simmer the cream sauce, reducing it until it thickens. Just before serving, add the apricot wedges to the sauce to heat. Return the breasts to the sauce to re-warm. Plate the breasts on the sided serving plate, pour the sauce over the top and serve.

* Pork loin medallions may also be used in this recipe without changing any other ingredients.

Chef's Notes

Swordfish en Mole

Serves 1

1 swordfish filet, about 10-12 ounces and 1 to 1½ inches thick

10 jumbo shrimp peeled, de-veined and tails removed

2 green onions diced

2 tablespoons roasted red bell pepper coarsely diced, Frieda's brand

1 clove garlic, minced

1 teaspoon olive oil

½ teaspoon cumin

2 cups water

1 cube KNORR® chicken bouillon

2 soup spoons DOÑA MARÍA® brand mole

Pinch of cayenne pepper

To Prepare:

Heat olive oil in a non-stick skillet over high heat. Dust the swordfish with cumin on both sides. Sear the fish on both sides, about two minutes each. Quickly add minced garlic and shrimp. Stir-fry for about one minute, just long enough to infuse the fish with garlic. Add water, bouillon, mole and cayenne pepper, reduce heat to medium, and simmer until thick, about four minutes. Add roasted bell peppers at the end, and heat them through. Remove from heat, transfer fish and shrimp to a serving dish, spoon sauce over the top, and garnish with green onions. Serve with hot white corn tortillas. Mexican rice is good with this too, if you have saved enough carbs for the day to include it.

Szechwan Grilled Salmon

Serves 1

1 filet of salmon, 10-12 ounces

1 teaspoon Szechwan Sauce, KA-ME brand

1 teaspoon Black Bean Sauce, KA-ME brand

1 teaspoon ground ginger, Spice World brand

1 tablespoon olive oil

1 teaspoon honey

1 clove garlic, minced

To Prepare:

Combine KA-ME Szechwan Sauce and Black Bean Sauce, ginger, olive oil, honey and ginger. Time provided, place the filet of salmon and the sauce together in a sealable bag and marinade prior to grilling for at least 30 minutes, or as long as overnight, in the refrigerator. Cook the salmon on both sides for about four to five minutes over a medium flame. You may add the remaining sauce from the bag over the fish as it cooks. If sticking is a problem, line the grill with some foil before cooking. Great over an open fire with a nonstick grill, grate or hand-held cooker. If you really like it hot, mix up more of the sauce to use as a condiment like ketchup.

* This recipe is also great with boneless, skinless chicken breast and requires no other substitutions of ingredients.

Chef's Notes

Tequila Lime Tilapia

Serves 2

2 filets golden tilapia

4 slices thick cut bacon sliced julienne ¼ inch strips

Juice of one lime

1 clove garlic, minced

2 tablespoons tequila

Tony Chachere's Original Creole Seasoning

To Prepare:

In a large non-stick skillet, brown the bacon strips. Remove browned bacon and set aside to drain on a paper towel. Pour off excess bacon grease, reserving one tablespoon in the skillet to fry the fish. Sprinkle Tony Chachere's Original Creole Seasoning over the fish on both sides. The amount is to your taste; I use it liberally. Sear the fish over medium-high heat until lightly golden on each side. Add the tequila, lime and garlic mixture to the skillet, and deglazing the fish on both sides. When the liquids get thick and bubbly, remove the fish from the pan, placing each piece on a serving plate. Pour the remaining liquids equally over the two pieces. Sprinkle with browned bacon and serve. You can also add a wedge of lime as a garnish. Yummy!!!

This is great with boneless skinless chicken breast too. To substitute chicken follow the recipe as stated with the exception of the cooking time, which should be increased.

Chef's Notes

Trote con Finocchio
Trout with Fennel

Serves 1

1 filet ruby trout, about 8-10 ounces

Ground white pepper to dust the fish

2 tablespoons butter

2 cloves garlic, minced divided

1 rib fennel, coarsely chopped, about ⅓ cup

½ cup dry vermouth

½ cube KNORR® chicken bouillon

2 Italian plumb tomatoes de-seeded and diced

2 pinches crushed red pepper

8 jumbo cocktail shrimp chopped coarsely, tails removed

½ teaspoon fresh dill weed chopped, dry will do

To Prepare:

In a non-stick skillet over medium heat, melt the butter. Lightly dust both sides of the trout filet with white pepper. Add the dusted filet to the skillet and pan-fry on one side until lightly golden, about three minutes. Turn the filet over to brown the other side, and add the chopped fennel to the skillet around the filet. While browning the second side, gently agitate the fennel with a wooden spoon to prevent it from being scorched. When the fish has browned on both sides, add the vermouth and the bouillon. Dissolve the bouillon in the wine, then add the tomatoes, shrimp, crushed red pepper and the chopped dill weed. Let the tomatoes cook a little, and the flavors of the dill and crushed pepper meld through by simmering for about two minutes. Carefully place the filet of trout on a serving plate and pour the rest of the skillet's contents over the top of the filet. Garnish with fresh fennel fronds and serve. Incredible flavor!

Chef's Notes

Tuna alla Putanesca

Serves 1

1 tuna steak, 10-12 ounces

1 large Italian plumb tomato de-seeded and diced medium

1 large clove garlic, minced and divided in half

¼ cup dry white wine or zinfandel for a sweeter taste

⅛ teaspoon white pepper, freshly ground

½ cube KNORR® chicken bouillon

2 small dried red chili peppers crumbled

2 tablespoons sweet unsalted butter

1 tablespoon black olives, sliced

To Prepare:

In a non-stick skillet, melt the butter over medium heat. Dust the tuna with white pepper on each side, about ¹⁄₁₆ of a teaspoon per side. Add half of the minced garlic to the skillet, warm it to emulsify, then sauté the tuna on one side until lightly golden, about three minutes. Add the other half clove of minced garlic to the pan, then turn tuna over and sauté the other side until golden. When both sides are lightly golden, add wine, chicken bouillon, tomato, crumbled chili peppers and olives. Reduce heat to medium and bring to a simmer, cook for two or more minutes, until the tomato forms a chunky sauce, and serve. Scrumptious and spicy!

* Chicken can very easily be substituted here without changing other ingredients. The same cooking techniques apply for chicken. The only exception is cooking time, about 5 minutes per side. Always cook chicken thoroughly.

Chef's Notes

Tuna Tacos Cancun Style

Serves 2

1 tuna steak 10-12 ounces

2 tablespoons butter, divided

½ teaspoon ground cumin, divided

1 clove garlic, minced, divided

Splash of fresh lime juice

6-8 corn tortillas

Olive oil

Mexican Slaw:

1 head romaine lettuce quartered and cut into ⅛ inch ribbons

2 Italian plumb tomatoes, diced finely

½ cup feta cheese, crumbled

2 tablespoons black beans, LA PREFERIDA® brand,
    washed and drained

Quarter the romaine lettuce and slice into ribbons like cold slaw about ⅛ inch wide. Combine the lettuce, tomatoes and feta cheese in a bowl, toss with the dressing.

Dressing:

¼ cup sour cream

2 tablespoons olive oil

5 tablespoons lime juice

1 tablespoon ground cumin

1 clove garlic, minced

Dash cayenne pepper

Fresh ground pepper to taste

In a two-cup measuring cup combine all of the ingredients together and whisk until smooth. Set aside until ready to serve.

To Prepare:

Melt one tablespoon of butter in a non-stick skillet over medium-high heat. Add half of the minced garlic and half of the cumin. Swirl ingredients to coat the pan. Add the tuna steak and sear on one side. Spread the remaining garlic, butter and cumin over the top of the steak as it cooks. Turn the steak in about four minutes and sear the other side. Tuna is best served with a lightly pink center. Remove the tuna from the skillet when done, and place on a serving plate. Cut the filet into ⅛ inch thick strips. Add a splash of fresh lime juice over the sliced tuna just before serving.

Tortillas:

Lightly drizzle olive oil between the tortillas and rub them together so that each tortilla has a light even coating. If you use too much oil, the tortillas will be greasy. Microwave on high for one minute, turning the tortillas halfway through. Fill the tortillas with sliced tuna steak and slaw. Try this with green salsa as a condiment; it's great!

Chef's Notes

_____

_____

_____

_____

_____

_____

_____

_____

_____

_____

_____

_____

Vegetables

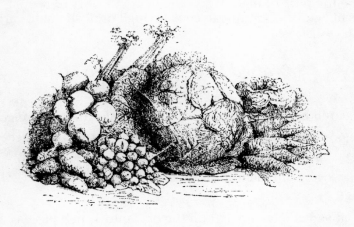

Braised Red and Yellow Peppers

Serves 2

2 large red bell peppers de-seeded and cut into ¼ inch thick julienne slices

2 large yellow bell peppers, de-seeded and cut into ¼ inch thick julienne slices

3 cloves garlic, minced

2 tablespoons olive oil

2 tablespoons white wine

½ cube KNORR® chicken bouillon

To Prepare:

In a non-stick skillet over medium heat, combine peppers and olive oil. Sauté until the peppers are tender, about six minutes. Increase the heat to high. When the peppers start to scorch, add the wine and garlic. Continue to cook on high until all liquids are evaporated, and serve.

Braised Vegetables Bistro Style

Serves 4

2 large red bell peppers, de-seeded and cut into 1 inch pieces

2 large yellow peppers, de-seeded and cut into 1 inch pieces

1 large red onion cut into wedges

1 large sweet onion cut into wedges

1 cup baby carrots

3 small stalks of celery cut on the bias into 1 inch pieces

1 bulb garlic cloves separated and minced

2 tablespoons honey

¼ cup red wine vinegar

¼ cup balsamic vinegar

1 cube KNORR® chicken bouillon

½ cup olive oil

½ teaspoon coarsely ground salt

1 ½ teaspoons ground black pepper

To Prepare:

In a large mixing bowl, combine the honey, red wine vinegar, balsamic vinegar, chicken bouillon, olive oil, salt and black pepper. Stir until the honey is dissolved. Add the vegetables and toss together in the liquids until evenly coated. Transfer the contents of the bowl to a large baking dish and place in a pre-heated 375-degree oven. Braise the vegetables in the oven uncovered for about 45 minutes or until the edges of the peppers and onions begin to brown a little. It is important to gently stir the vegetables once or twice while braising, to ensure that they get evenly cooked. This recipe is great as above, but if you like fennel, try adding a bulb, cut into one inch pieces. Really scrumptious!

Chef's Notes

Broccoli Floret's Steamed with Lemon

Serves 4

1 head broccoli separated into florets, stems peeled and sliced about ⅛ inch thick on the bias, diagonally.

4 tablespoons butter

Juice of 1 lemon

To Prepare:

In a large covered skilled over high heat, melt the butter. Add the broccoli florets and sliced stems. Cover and vigorously shake skillet over the heat for two or three minutes. Add the lemon juice to the pan and cover again, steaming the broccoli for about two minutes. Serve immediately. This dish is quick and very good.

Broccoli with Herbed Butter

Serves 2

1 pound broccoli florets

½ stick butter

½ teaspoon basil

½ teaspoon oregano

½ teaspoon marjoram

2 cloves garlic, minced

To Prepare:

In a small saucepan, melt the butter over low heat, with care not to burn it. Add the basil, oregano, marjoram and garlic. Let the herbs warm through the butter for about one minute to let all of the flavors meld and emulsify. Remove the pan from the heat and set aside.

Steam the broccoli in ½ cup of water in a large pan until bright green and slightly tender. Drain the broccoli well. Pour the herbed butter over the broccoli, cover and toss together, and serve immediately.

* Parmesan cheese sprinkled over the top or melted mozzarella poured over the top before serving is great too.

Chef's Notes

Brussels Sprouts Braised with Onions and Chestnuts

Serves 2

1 pound fresh or frozen Brussels sprouts

3 tablespoons butter

1 tablespoon olive oil

1 large sweet onion, diced medium

1 cup chestnuts hulled peeled and sliced thick

²⁄₃ cup mead, a wine made from honey

1 cube KNORR® chicken bouillon

To Prepare:

In a heavy stockpot, melt the butter in one tablespoon of olive oil over medium heat. Add the diced onion and sauté until transparent, about three minutes. Add the Brussels sprouts and gently stir them. Sauté until they are bright green and the onions have begun to golden, about four minutes. Add the chestnuts, wine and chicken bouillon. Increase the heat to medium-high, bringing the liquids to a strong simmer. Continue to simmer, stirring frequently, to avoid scorching the Brussels sprouts until the liquids reduce to a glaze. Remove from heat and transfer to a serving bowl and serve immediately. You are better off not to let them cool as Brussels sprouts have a tendency to become bitter as they cool. If you've never liked Brussels sprouts before, I think you will like these... they are really delicious.

Cauliflower Augratin

Serves 1 to 2

1 tablespoon olive oil

1 clove garlic, minced

1 pound frozen cauliflower

¼ cup white zinfandel wine

1 cube KNORR® chicken bouillon

4 ounces brie cheese, crust removed

¼ cup heavy whipping cream

2 tablespoons Parmesan cheese, freshly grated is best here

½ cup gruyere cheese, grated

One pinch fresh ground nutmeg, 3-4 scratches with a grater

½ cup Caesar croutons crushed, finishes the dish nicely if you
    have the carbs to spare

To Prepare:

In an oven-safe skillet, heat the olive oil. Add garlic and cauliflower and sauté over medium heat, gently stirring frequently until cauliflower is lightly golden, about four minutes. Add wine and bouillon. When the bouillon has dissolved, add the brie cheese and whipping cream. When the cheese melts and the sauce has formed, stir in two or three turns of black pepper and the nutmeg, freshly ground. Remove from heat and sprinkle Parmesan cheese over the top. Next, spread the grated gruyere cheese evenly over the top. If you're using the croutons, measure them: $\frac{1}{2}$ cup before crushing them. Sprinkle crushed croutons over the top, bake in a pre-heated 475-degree oven for 15-20 minutes or when the top is lightly golden. WOW!!!

Chef's Notes

_____

_____

_____

_____

_____

_____

_____

_____

_____

_____

_____

_____

Cavolfiore al Forno
Oven Roasted Cauliflower with Cheese

Serves 2

1 pound cauliflower florets

4 scallions, whites finely chopped, greens sliced thin

⅓ cup olive oil

3 cloves garlic, minced

½ teaspoon fresh ground black pepper

1 cube KNORR® chicken bouillon

½ cup white zinfandel wine

½ cup Parmesan cheese divided; use canned in this case

To Prepare:

In a large mixing bowl combine the cauliflower, white part of the scallions, olive oil, garlic, black pepper and half of the Parmesan cheese. In a microwave-safe cup, combine the wine and bouillon cube, and heat on high in the microwave to dissolve the bouillon, about 45 seconds to one minute. Add the wine and dissolved bouillon to the mixing bowl. Stir the ingredients together well, making sure to evenly and thoroughly coat the cauliflower. Transfer the contents of the mixing bowl to an 8 by 12 inch baking dish. Place the baking dish in a pre-heated 400-degree oven and bake until the cauliflower begins to become a little golden, about 20 minutes. Remove the dish from the oven. Sprinkle the remaining Parmesan cheese over the cauliflower and add the greens of the scallions at this point. Gently toss the cheese and scallion greens into the cauliflower mixture in the baking dish, and return it to the oven for another 10-15 minutes or until the top of the cauliflower is nicely golden. Remove from the oven and serve. This dish is great; it can be prepared up to a day in advance, and kept in the fridge before baking. An easy and elegant choice for a dinner party, but you will need to double the recipe for four people.

Chef's Notes

Chilled Green Bean Bundles Vinaigrette

Serves 4

1 pound fresh green beans, ends snipped

½ pound prosciuto; if not available try thinly sliced Virginia ham

Vinaigrette:

½ cup extra virgin olive oil

⅓ cup red wine vinegar

2 cloves garlic, minced

1 teaspoon fresh black pepper, crushed / milled coarsely

To Prepare:

Steam the green beans until done but still crisp, about four minutes. Drain and cool the beans by running cold water over them as soon as they are done. Divide the beans into six equal bundles, about 1½ to 2 inches in diameter. Wrap the bundles with sliced prosciuto or ham, one slice each, tightly. Place the bundles in an airtight sealable plastic container. Pour the vinaigrette over the bundles. Cover and chill in the refrigerator. Turn the bundles (or the container, if it seals tightly enough) every couple of hours. Chill for at least six hours before serving. Best prepared the night before and turned frequently through the next day. A little time consuming, but a delicious show-stopper for a vegetable entrée. This is a wonderful dish for hot summer days when a hot vegetable is less appealing.

Finocchio alla Campagnola
Fennel Italian Country Style

Serves 1 to 2

4 cups fennel stalks cut into 1 inch pieces

1 cup baby Lima beans

2 tablespoons fennel fronds reserve for garnish

6 strips thick cut bacon cut into ½ inch strips

1 medium onion diced finely

2 large cloves garlic

1 cube KNORR® chicken bouillon

½ cup white wine

To Prepare:

Fry the bacon in a large non-stick skillet until brown and chewy not crisp. Remove the bacon from the pan and reserve for later. Add fennel, onion, Lima beans and one clove of minced garlic to the bacon drippings. Sauté until the vegetables are half done, about four minutes. Add the wine, bouillon and the last clove of minced garlic. Sauté until the liquids have almost evaporated, two to three minutes. Toss in the bacon and stir. Add the fronds of the fennel over the top to garnish. Cover and set aside for two to three minutes to brighten the fronds, then serve. Fennel has the most unique properties: it smells like licorice, but has a wonderful flavor when cooked. Fennel is great raw too. Try using it in salads.

Chef's Notes

Fresh Green Beans with Toasted Almonds

Serves 1 to 2

1 pound fresh green beans, or cut fresh frozen green beans

1 cube KNORR® chicken bouillon

1 cup water

½ cup slivered almonds

4 tablespoons butter

To Prepare:

Bring one cup of water to a boil in a large saucepan. Add bouillon and beans. Boil for four to five minutes until done, but still crisp. While the beans are cooking, melt the butter over medium heat in a non-stick skillet. Add almonds, stirring constantly to avoid burning the butter. Toast the almonds to a golden brown. When beans are done, drain well and transfer into the skillet with almonds. Toss together and serve. Simple, quick and delicious!

Fried Cabbage Gypsy Style

Serves 4

1 head cabbage core removed and cut into 1½ inch squares

1 large sweet onion cut into thin wedges

6 slices thick cut bacon cut into ½ inch strips

1 teaspoon Tony Chachere's Original Creole Seasoning

1 tablespoon black pepper

⅛ teaspoon cayenne pepper

1 ½ tablespoons hot sauce

Olive oil for frying

To Prepare:

Fry the bacon in a large non-stick pan (preferably one with tall sides like a chicken fryer) until browned but not crisp. Remove the bacon from the pan, allowing it to drain on paper toweling. Reserve the bacon drippings in the pan. Add the cabbage and sweet onion to the hot bacon drippings. Fry the cabbage and sweet onion, adding the Tony Chachere's Original Creole Seasoning, black pepper and cayenne pepper as you stir-fry the cabbage and onions. Continue to stir-fry until the onions are translucent and the cabbage is bright green but tender, about six minutes. Add only enough Olive oil to prevent the vegetables from sticking and burning. Add the hot sauce at the end, just as the cabbage is reducing in bulk and becoming tender. Stir-fry for an additional two or three minutes after adding the hot sauce. Add the fried bacon to the cabbage just as it is getting done. Serve while hot, and be careful – this stuff is spicy, Yuoi brey!

Chef's Notes

_____

_____

_____

_____

_____

_____

_____

_____

_____

_____

_____

_____

_____

Green Beans Parmegianno

Serves 1 to 2

1 pound fresh or frozen green beans

6 slices thick cut bacon sliced into $\frac{1}{2}$ inch wide strips

$\frac{3}{4}$ cup Parmesan cheese

To Prepare:

Fry the bacon until brown but not crisp. Remove the bacon from the pan and set aside, allowing the bacon to drain while you bring the green beans to boil in another pan. Reserve one tablespoon of the bacon drippings for the beans. When the green beans come to a boil, allow them to cook for a couple of minutes until done, but still crisp.

Drain the green beans well, return them to the pan, and add the bacon drippings and Parmesan cheese. Toss the beans, bacon and Parmesan together, making sure that the cheese coats evenly, then serve. This is probably one of the easiest and most delicious ways to serve green beans that I've ever tried.

Lima Beans Fazule

Serves 4

2 cups baby Lima beans

1 cup dry white wine

2 cloves garlic, minced

1 cube KNORR® chicken bouillon

3 slices thick cut bacon, cut into $\frac{1}{2}$ inch strips

$\frac{1}{2}$ cup Parmesan cheese

To Prepare:

In a non-stick pan, fry the bacon until browned and chewy, but not crisp. Remove the bacon from the pan and set aside to drain on paper toweling. Add the Lima beans to the bacon drippings with one clove of minced garlic. Sauté over medium-high heat for four to five minutes. Add the wine and bouillon to the pan. Reduce the heat to medium, and simmer until almost all of the liquid has evaporated. Add the bacon and the last clove of minced garlic. Stir the bacon into the beans and cook for two or three more minutes. Remove the pan from the stove and sprinkle Parmesan cheese over the top. Cover and let stand for two or three minutes before serving. Due to the higher carbohydrate content of Lima beans, this should be served in $\frac{1}{2}$ cup portions.

Chef's Notes

Minted Baby Lima Beans

Serves 2

1 cup baby Lima beans

½ medium, sweet onion, finely diced

2 strips thick cut bacon, sliced into ½ inch strips

½ cube KNORR® chicken bouillon

½ cup white zinfandel wine

1 tablespoon fresh mint chopped coarsely

To Prepare:

In a non-stick skillet, fry the bacon until browned and chewy, but not crisp. Remove the bacon from the pan and drain on paper toweling. Add the onion and baby Lima beans to the bacon drippings and stir-fry until the onions become translucent. Add the wine and bouillon, reduce heat to medium and simmer reducing the fluids almost completely until the beans are glazed. Add the mint and cook for another one to two minutes to release the mint flavor. Add the bacon, stir, then serve. Unusually good!!!

Oven Roasted Turnips Italian Style

Serves 4

8-10 large turnips, peeled and cut into ¼ inch cubes

½ cup olive oil

6 cloves garlic, minced

1 teaspoon oregano

1 teaspoon marjoram

1 teaspoon rosemary leaves, fresh is best here

½ cup grated Parmesan cheese, canned pre-grated variety

To Prepare:

In a large bowl, combine turnips, olive oil, minced garlic, oregano, marjoram and rosemary, and toss well. Coat the turnip cubes evenly, add the Parmesan cheese and toss well again, coating the turnips evenly with the cheese. Transfer this mixture to a large baking dish and bake, uncovered, at 450-degrees for 45 minutes to an hour or until the turnips are golden. Remember to stir the turnips two or three times while broasting, to ensure that they brown evenly. This dish is an incredible substitute for a potato, and easy on the carbohydrates too. Turnips have virtually no carbohydrates. Enjoy!

Chef's Notes

Parsleyed Turnips

Serves 4

3 large turnips peeled and cut into ½ inch cubes

4 tablespoons butter

2 tablespoons fresh chopped Italian parsley

1 cube KNORR® chicken bouillon

2 tablespoons of water reserved from boiling turnips

To Prepare:

Place the cubed turnips in a large saucepan. Add just enough water to the pan to cover the turnips. Bring the turnips to a boil and reduce the heat to a strong simmer. Simmer the turnips until tender, about eight minutes. While the turnips are cooking, remove two tablespoons of the water from the pan. Add the chicken bouillon to the two reserved tablespoons of water and dissolve the bouillon. When tender, pour the turnips into a strainer to drain. Return the saucepan to the stove and melt the butter. When the butter has melted, add the turnips, parsley and the dissolved bouillon to the saucepan. Toss together gently, with care not to break up the turnips, and serve. This is another great potato substitute. Try serving this with Roast Chicken, Italian Style on page 144. Delicious!

Piselli Con Cipolla
Peas and Onions Italian Style

Serves 4 to 6

1 pound fresh, frozen green peas

2 tablespoons olive oil

1 medium yellow onion, diced medium to fine

½ cup white wine, dry to medium dry

1 cube KNORR® chicken bouillon

To Prepare:

In a large saucepan over medium-high heat, add olive oil. Bring to temperature and add onions. Sauté until the onions are transparent. Add peas and sauté together, stirring constantly, until the peas are bright green, about four minutes. Add the wine and chicken bouillon, reduce the heat to medium and slowly simmer. Cook the peas and onions, stirring occasionally, until the liquids evaporate and the peas are a little glazed, about eight to ten minutes. This very traditional Italian dish is great with chicken, pork and fish.

Chef's Notes

Savory Beans

Serves 1 to 2

2 cups Italian fava beans, cut or whole
These are flat Italian green beans.

4 slices thick cut lean bacon cut into ½ inch strips

½ cup baby Lima beans

1 medium sweet onion cut into thin wedges

2 cloves garlic, minced

½ cube KNORR® chicken bouillon

2 tablespoons white wine

1 teaspoon savory leaves

To Prepare:

In a non-stick pan over medium-high heat, fry the bacon until browned but not crunchy. Remove the fried bacon from the pan and set aside to drain on paper toweling. Reserve two tablespoons of the bacon drippings in the pan to sauté the beans. Add the fava beans, Lima beans, onion and one clove of minced garlic. Sauté until the onions begin to brown on the edges about four minutes. Add the wine and chicken bouillon. Sauté until the liquids reduce to glaze the beans. Add the last clove of minced garlic and the savory leaves. Stir for about two minutes and serve. These beans are hearty and flavorful enough to be a meal by themselves. They go really well with Seared Peppercorn Salmon with Bourbon Honey Glaze, pages 160-161.

Sugar Snap Peas with Caramelized Onions

Serves 2

1 pound sugar snap peas

1 large sweet onion diced medium

3 tablespoons butter, divided

2 tablespoons red wine vinegar

1 clove garlic, minced

1 teaspoon brown sugar

1 cube KNORR® chicken bouillon

To Prepare:

In a non-stick pan, melt two tablespoons of butter over medium heat. Add onions and sauté, with care not to burn the butter, while bringing the onions to a golden color on the edges. Add wine vinegar, bouillon and minced garlic. Simmer for about one minute, just long enough to infuse the garlic. Add the brown sugar, combine until melted, and remove from heat. Steam the sugar snap peas in a separate pan until just tender, about four minutes. Drain well. Toss with caramelized onions and the third tablespoon of butter, and serve.

Chef's Notes

Summer Vegetables Misto

Serves 2 to 4

2 small zucchini, quartered and sliced thin

1 small yellow summer squash, quartered and sliced thin

1 large sweet onion, cut into wedges

3 Italian plumb tomatoes, de-seeded and diced medium

5 large cloves garlic, minced

1 cube KNORR® chicken bouillon

2 tablespoons white zinfandel wine

¾ to 1 cup grated Parmesan cheese, can variety

2 tablespoons olive oil

To Prepare:

In a large skillet over medium-high heat, warm the olive oil. Add two cloves of garlic. Add zucchini, squash and onion. Sauté until zucchini and squash are heated through, about four minutes. In a microwave, heat the wine and bouillon to dissolve the bouillon cube. Add tomatoes, wine and bouillon mixture, and remaining minced garlic to the skillet. Sauté until the liquids evaporate, about two minutes. Remove the skillet from the heat and sprinkle Parmesan cheese over the top. Cover the skillet and set aside for five minutes to melt the cheese before serving. This is a wonderful medley of flavors that complements almost anything that you can throw on the grill.

Chef's Notes

Culinary Dictionary

Boil: to keep a liquid at a temperature that produces bubbles breaking the surface of the liquid.

Chop: to cut food into irregular pieces approximately the size of a pea.

Chop Coarsely: to cut food into irregular pieces approximately the size of pistachio nutmeats.

Chop fine; to cut food in to irregular pieces approximately the size of a grain of rice.

Deglaze: to dissolve the residue resulting from searing, frying or browning foods on the bottom of a cooking pan by adding a liquid and bringing to a boil while stirring. The result is then used as a foundation for a sauce or gravy.

Dice: to cut food into square pieces uniformly approximately $\frac{1}{8}$ to $\frac{1}{4}$ inch in size.

Julienne: to cut food into uniform long pieces like straws or ribbons.

Poach: to cook wrapped, or otherwise contained food by simmering submerged in a liquid.

Purée: to blend foods, mostly fruits and vegetables, in a food processor or blender until they form a smooth sauce.

Reduce: to boil a liquid solution allowing evaporation to the point that the original solution becomes concentrated in thickness and flavor.

Sauté: to quickly fry foods in a small amount of fat over moderately high to high heat.

Simmer: to keep a liquid at a temperature just below boiling so that the liquid trembles.

Steam: to cook foods by using the vapors, which rise from boiling liquids in an enclosed vessel such as a covered pan.

Index of Recipes

Product and Ingredient Resources

To insure your success in "cooking yourself skinny," you must first take a hard look at your refrigerator, freezer, cupboards and pantry. Read all of the labels. If foods are sugar-laden or loaded with carbohydrates, *throw them out!*

I have listed the specialty ingredients in the recipes and where to find them in the index below. Should you find that you don't have access to the products I have listed, or your grocery store doesn't carry a particular item, ask the manager to see if they can order the item for you.

Anchovy Paste: **Giovanni's Appetizing Food Products** brand. Look in the aisle where canned tuna is stocked or contact Giovanni's at 1-586-727-9355.

Black Beans: **LA PREFERIDA®** brand. Look in the Mexican food section, or contact LA PREFERIDA® directly at 1-773-254-7200.

Chicken, Beef, Fish, Vegetable and Shrimp Bouillon: **KNORR®** brand. Look in the soup section of your supermarket and in the Mexican food section, or call 1-800-338-8831.

Chipotle Peppers in Adobo Sauce: **HERDEZ®** brand. Look in the Mexican food section of your grocery store or online at www.herdez.com.

Chocolate: **Pure De-lite Belgian Chocolate.** For availability and retail stores near you call Pure De-lite Belgian Chocolate at 1-866-4LOCARB.

Extra Hot Pure Horseradish: **Woeber's** brand. Look in the meat case by the ham or online at www.woebersmustard.com or customer service at 1-800-548-2929.

Ground Ginger: **Spice World** brand. Look in the prepared salad refrigerator case in the fresh produce section, or online at www.spiceworldinc.com or customer service at 1-407-851-9432.

Italian Bread Crumbs: **PROGRESSO** brand from **General Mills Inc.** PROGRESSO is a registered trademark of Pet Incorporated. Look in the baking aisle of your supermarket, online at www.genmills.com or call 1-800-200-9377.

Mexican Green Sauce/ Salsa Verde : HERDEZ® brand. Look in the Mexican food section of your grocery store, or online at www.herdez.com.

Mole: DOÑA MARÍA® brand. Look in the Mexican food section, or online at www.worldfood.com.

Pancakes, Waffles, Hot Cereal, Granola and Pizza Crust Mix: **LowCarb Success** brand. Available online at www.lowcarbsuccess.org.

Peach and Apricot Nectar: **Del Valle Nectars** Brand, from **Jugos Del Valle U.S.A. Inc.** Look in the Mexican food section of your grocery store, call at 1-888-349-2234 or order online at www.vallenectars.com.

Roasted Red Bell Peppers: **Frieda's Inc.** brand. Look in the prepared salad refrigerator case in the fresh produce section, online at www.friedas.com, or phone customer service at 1-800-241-1771.

Seasoning: **Tony Chachere's Original Creole Seasoning.** Look in the spices and seasonings aisle at your supermarket, online at www.tonychachere.com or call Tony's Consumer hotline at 1-800-551-9066.

Sesame Oil and Select Hot Oil: **China Bowl** brand. Look in the Oriental food section or contact China Bowl directly at 1-203-222-0381.

Snacks: **Just The Cheese Crunchy, Baked Cheese Snacks from Specialty Cheese Company Inc.** Look in the Natural food section, online at www.specialcheese.com or call 1-800-367-1711.

Sugar Free Jams: **Estee** brand. Look in the sugar free/ Diabetic foods section, online at www.esteefoods.com or or by phone at 1-800-434-4246 and ask for customer service.

Sweetener: SPLENDA™ *Granular* brand. Look in the Diabetic and sugar free foods section, www.splenda.com or call 1-800-777-5363.

Szechuan Sauce, Hoisin Sauce and Black Bean Sauce: I use only **KA-ME** brand. Look in the Oriental food section. You can contact the distributor, Liberty Richter division of Tree of Life, online at www.libertyrichter.com or by phone at 1-201-843-8900.

Quick Reference Carb/Fiber & Protein Chart

The following chart was adapted from the USDA Nutrient Database, Release 13, Compostion of Foods.

Food Description	Nutrient	Limit 50 gm/D Carbohydrate/wt gm/100 gm	20-30 gm/D Fiber/wt gm/100 gm	45-63 gm/D Protein/wt gm/100 gm
BUTTER, WITH & WITHOUT SALT		0.06	0.0	0.9
CHEESE, BLUE		2.34	0.0	21.4
CHEESE, BRICK		2.79	0.0	23.2
CHEESE, BRIE		0.45	0.0	20.8
CHEESE, CAMEMBERT		0.46	0.0	19.8
CHEESE, CARAWAY		3.06	0.0	25.2
CHEESE, CHEDDAR		1.28	0.0	24.9
CHEESE, CHESHIRE		4.78	0.0	23.4
CHEESE, COLBY		2.57	0.0	23.8
CHEESE, COTTAGE, CRMD, LRG OR SML CURD		2.68	0.0	12.5
CHEESE, COTTAGE, NONFAT, UNCRMD, DRY, LRG OR SML CURD		1.85	0.0	17.3
CHEESE, COTTAGE, LOWFAT, 2% MILKFAT		3.63	0.0	13.7
CHEESE, COTTAGE, LOWFAT, 1% MILKFAT		2.72	0.0	12.4
CHEESE, CREAM		2.66	0.0	7.6
CHEESE, EDAM		1.43	0.0	25.0
CHEESE, FETA		4.09	0.0	14.2
CHEESE, FONTINA		1.55	0.0	25.6
CHEESE, GJETOST		42.65	0.0	9.7
CHEESE, GOUDA		2.22	0.0	24.9
CHEESE, GRUYERE		0.36	0.0	29.8
CHEESE, LIMBURGER		0.49	0.0	20.1
CHEESE, MONTEREY		0.68	0.0	24.5
CHEESE, MOZZARELLA, WHL MILK		2.22	0.0	19.4
CHEESE, MOZZARELLA, WHL MILK, LO MOIST		2.47	0.0	21.6
CHEESE, MOZZARELLA, PART SKIM MILK		2.77	0.0	24.3
CHEESE, MOZZARELLA, PART SKIM MILK, LO MOIST		3.14	0.0	27.5
CHEESE, MUENSTER		1.12	0.0	23.4
CHEESE, NEUFCHATEL		2.94	0.0	10.0
CHEESE, PARMESAN, GRATED		3.74	0.0	41.6
CHEESE, PARMESAN, HARD		3.22	0.0	35.8
CHEESE, PORT DE SALUT		0.57	0.0	23.8
CHEESE, PROVOLONE		2.14	0.0	25.6
CHEESE, RICOTTA, WHOLE MILK		3.04	0.0	11.3
CHEESE, RICOTTA, PART SKIM MILK		5.14	0.0	11.4
CHEESE, ROMANO		3.63	0.0	31.8
CHEESE, ROQUEFORT		2	0.0	21.5
CHEESE, SWISS		3.38	0.0	28.4
CHEESE, TILSIT		1.88	0.0	24.4
CHEESE, PAST PROCESS, AMERICAN, W/DI NA PO4		1.6	0.0	22.2
CHEESE, PAST PROCESS, PIMENTO		1.73	0.0	22.1
CHEESE, PAST PROCESS, SWISS, W/DI NA PO4		2.1	0.0	24.7

Food Description	Nutrient	Limit 50 gm/D Carbohydrate/wt gm/100 gm	20-30 gm/D Fiber/wt gm/100 gm	45-63 gm/D Protein/wt gm/100 gm
CHEESE FD, COLD PK, AMERICAN		8.32	0.0	19.7
CHEESE FD, PAST PROCESS, AMERICAN, WO/DI NA PO4		7.29	0.0	19.6
CHEESE FD, PAST PROCESS, SWISS		4.5	0.0	21.9
CHEESE, GOAT, HARD TYPE		2.17	0.0	30.5
CHEESE, GOAT, SEMISOFT TYPE		2.54	0.0	21.6
CHEESE, GOAT, SOFT TYPE		0.89	0.0	18.5
CHEESE SUB, MOZZARELLA		23.67	0.0	11.5
CHEESE, MEXICAN, QUESO ANEJO		4.63	0.0	21.4
CHEESE, MEXICAN, QUESO ASADERO		2.87	0.0	22.6
CHEESE, MEXICAN, QUESO CHIHUAHUA		5.56	0.0	21.6
CHEESE, LOFAT, CHEDDAR OR COLBY		1.91	0.0	24.4
CHEESE, LOW-SODIUM, CHEDDAR OR COLBY		1.91	0.0	24.4
CHEESE, CREAM, FAT FREE		5.8	0.0	14.4
CHEESE SPRD, PAST PROCESS, AMERICAN, WO/DI NA PO4		8.73	0.0	16.4
CREAM, FLUID, HALF AND HALF		4.3	0.0	3.0
CREAM, FLUID, LT WHIPPING		2.96	0.0	2.2
CREAM, FLUID, HVY WHIPPING		2.79	0.0	2.1
CREAM, WHIPPED, CRM TOPPING, PRESSURIZED		12.49	0.0	3.2
CREAM, SOUR, RED FAT, CULTURED		4.26	0.0	2.9
CREAM, SOUR, CULTURED		4.27	0.0	3.2
EGGNOG		13.54	0.0	3.8
SOUR DRSNG, NON-BUTTERFAT, CULTURED, FILLED CREAM-TYPE		4.68	0.0	3.3
SOUR CRM, IMITN, CULTURED		6.63	0.0	2.4
MILK, FLUID, 3.25% MILKFAT		4.66	0.0	3.3
MILK, PRODUCER, FLUID, 3.7% MILKFAT		4.65	0.0	3.3
MILK, RED FAT, FLUID, 2% MILKFAT, W/ VIT A		4.8	0.0	3.3
MILK, RED FAT, FLUID, 2% MILKFAT, W/ NONFAT MILK SOL&VIT A		4.97	0.0	3.5
MILK, RED FAT, FLUID, 2% MILKFAT, PROT FORT, W/ VIT A		5.49	0.0	4.0
MILK, LOWFAT, FLUID, 1% MILKFAT, W/ VIT A		4.78	0.0	3.3
MILK, LOWFAT, FLUID, 1% MILKFAT, W/ NONFAT MILK SOL&VIT A		4.97	0.0	3.5
MILK, LOWFAT, FLUID, 1% MILKFAT, PROT FORT, W/ VIT A		5.52	0.0	3.9
MILK, NONFAT, FLUID, W/ VIT A (FAT FREE OR SKIM)		4.85	0.0	3.4
MILK, NONFAT, FLUID, W/ NONFAT MILK SOL&VIT A (FAT FREE/SKIM)		5.02	0.0	3.6
MILK, NONFAT, FLUID, PROT FORT, W/ VIT A (FAT FREE/SKIM)		5.56	0.0	4.0
MILK, BTTRMLK, FLUID, CULTURED, LOWFAT		4.79	0.0	3.3
MILK, LOW SODIUM, FLUID		4.46	0.0	3.1
MILK, GOAT, FLUID		4.45	0.0	3.6
SOY MILK, FLUID		1.81	1.3	2.8
TOFU, FIRM, PREP W/CA SULFATE&MAGNESIUM CHLORIDE (NIGARI)		2.97	0.4	8.0
TOFU, SOFT, PREP W/CA SULFATE&MAGNESIUM CHLORIDE (NIGARI)		1.8	0.2	6.6
TOFU, DRIED-FROZEN (KOYADOFU)		14.56	7.2	47.9
TOFU, FRIED		10.5	3.9	17.2
TOFU, OKARA		12.54	0.0	3.2
TOFU, SALTED&FERMENTED (FUYU)		5.15	0.0	8.2

Food Description	Nutrient	Limit 50 gm/D Carbohydrate/wt gm/100 gm	20-30 gm/D Fiber/wt gm/100 gm	45-63 gm/D Protein/wt gm/100 gm
YOGURT, PLN, WHL MILK, 8 GRAMS PROT PER 8 OZ		4.66	0.0	3.5
YOGURT, PLN, LOFAT, 12 GRAMS PROT PER 8 OZ		7.04	0.0	5.3
YOGURT, PLN, SKIM MILK, 13 GRAMS PROT PER 8 OZ		7.68	0.0	5.7
EGG, WHOLE, RAW, FRESH		1.22	0.0	12.5
EGG, WHITE, RAW, FRESH		1.03	0.0	10.5
EGG, YOLK, RAW, FRESH		1.78	0.0	16.8
EGG, WHOLE, COOKED, FRIED		1.36	0.0	13.5
EGG, WHL, CKD, HARD-BOILED		1.12	0.0	12.6
EGG, WHOLE, COOKED, OMELET		1.04	0.0	10.3
EGG, WHOLE, COOKED, POACHED		1.22	0.0	12.4
EGG, WHL, CKD, SCRMBLD		2.2	0.0	11.1
EGG SUBSTITUTE, FROZEN		3.2	0.0	11.3
EGG SUBSTITUTE, LIQUID		0.64	0.0	12.0
SALAD DRSNG, RUSSIAN, W/SALT		10.4	0.0	1.6
SALAD DRSNG, 1000 ISLAND, COMM, REG, W/SALT		15.2	0.0	0.9
SALAD DRSNG, MAYO TYPE, REG, W/SALT		23.9	0.0	0.9
SALAD DRSNG, FRENCH, DIET, LOFAT, 5 CAL PER TSP, W/SALT		21.7	0.0	0.2
SALAD DRSNG, ITALIAN, COMM, DIET, 2 CAL PER TSP, W/SALT		4.9	0.1	0.1
SALAD DRSNG, RUSSIAN, LO CAL, W/SALT		27.6	0.3	0.5
SALAD DRSNG, 1000 ISLAND, DIET, LO CAL, 10 CAL PER TSP, W/SALT		16.2	1.2	0.8
BARBECUE LOAF, PORK, BEEF		6.4	0.0	15.8
BOLOGNA, BEEF		0.8	0.0	12.2
BOLOGNA, BEEF AND PORK		2.79	0.0	11.7
BOLOGNA, PORK		0.73	0.0	15.3
BOLOGNA, TURKEY		0.97	0.0	13.7
CHICKEN ROLL, LIGHT MEAT		2.45	0.0	19.5
CORNED BEEF LOAF, JELLIED		0	0.0	22.9
HAM, SLICED, EX LN, (APPROX 5% FAT)		0.97	0.0	19.4
HAM, SLICED, REG (APPROX 11% FAT)		3.11	0.0	17.6
HAM SALAD SPREAD		10.65	0.0	8.7
HAM&CHS LOAF OR ROLL		1.43	0.0	16.6
HEADCHEESE, PORK		0.3	0.0	16.0
HONEY LOAF, PORK, BEEF		5.33	0.0	15.8
KIELBASA, KOLBASSY, PORK, BF, NONFAT DRY MILK		2.14	0.0	13.3
LIVER CHEESE, PORK		2.1	0.0	15.2
LIVER SAUSAGE, LIVERWURST, PORK		2.2	0.0	14.1
LUNCHEON MEAT, BEEF, LOAVED		2.9	0.0	14.4
LUNCHEON MEAT, BF, THIN SLICED		5.71	0.0	28.1
LUNCHEON MEAT, PORK, CANNED		2.1	0.0	12.5
LUNCHEON MEAT, PORK, BEEF		2.33	0.0	12.6
MORTADELLA, BEEF, PORK		3.05	0.0	16.4
OLIVE LOAF, PORK		9.2	0.0	11.8
PASTRAMI, TURKEY		1.66	0.0	18.4
PATE, CHICKEN LIVER, CANNED		6.55	0.0	13.5
PATE, GOOSE LIVER, SMOKED, CND		4.67	0.0	11.4

Food Description	Nutrient	Limit 50 gm/D Carbohydrate/wt gm/100 gm	20-30 gm/D Fiber/wt gm/100 gm	45-63 gm/D Protein/wt gm/100 gm
PATE, LIVER, NOT SPECIFIED, CND		1.5	0.0	14.2
PEPPERED LOAF, PORK, BEEF		4.6	0.0	17.3
PEPPERONI, PORK, BEEF		2.84	0.0	21.0
PICKLE&PIMIENTO LOAF, PORK		5.9	0.0	11.5
LUXURY LOAF, PORK		4.9	0.0	18.4
MOTHER'S LOAF, PORK		7.53	0.0	12.1
PICNIC LOAF, PORK, BEEF		4.76	0.0	14.9
SALAMI, COOKED, BEEF		2.81	0.0	15.0
SALAMI, CKD, BF&PORK		2.25	0.0	13.9
SALAMI, COOKED, TURKEY		0.55	0.0	16.4
SALAMI, DRY OR HARD, PORK		1.6	0.0	22.6
SALAMI, DRY OR HARD, PORK, BF		2.59	0.0	22.9
TURKEY BREAST MEAT		0	0.0	22.5
TURKEY HAM, CURED TURKEY THIGH MEAT		0.37	0.0	18.9
TURKEY ROLL, LIGHT MEAT		0.53	0.0	18.7
TURKEY ROLL, LT&DK MEAT		2.13	0.0	18.1
HONEY ROLL SAUSAGE, BEEF		2.18	0.0	18.6
APPLES, RAW, WITH SKIN		15.25	2.7	0.2
APPLES, RAW, WITHOUT SKIN		14.84	1.9	0.2
APPLES, RAW, WO/SKN, CKD, BLD		13.64	2.4	0.3
APPLES, RAW, WO/SKN, CKD, MICROWAVE		14.41	2.8	0.3
APRICOTS, RAW		11.12	2.4	1.4
AVOCADOS, RAW, ALL COMM VAR		7.39	5.0	2.0
AVOCADOS, RAW, CALIFORNIA		6.91	4.9	2.1
AVOCADOS, RAW, FLORIDA		8.91	5.3	1.6
BANANAS, RAW		23.43	2.4	1.0
BLACKBIES, RAW		12.76	5.3	0.7
BLACKBIES, FRZ, UNSWTND		15.67	5.0	1.2
BLUEBIES, RAW		14.13	2.7	0.7
BLUEBIES, FRZ, UNSWTND		12.17	2.7	0.4
BOYSENBIES, FRZ, UNSWTND		12.19	3.9	1.1
CARAMBOLA, (STARFRUIT), RAW		7.83	2.7	0.5
CHIES, SOUR, RED, RAW		12.18	1.6	1.0
CRANBIES, RAW		12.68	4.2	0.4
CURRANTS, EUROPEAN BLACK, RAW		15.38	0.0	1.4
CURRANTS, RED&WHITE, RAW		13.8	4.3	1.4
DATES, DOMESTIC, NAT&DRY		73.51	7.5	2.0
FIGS, RAW		19.18	3.3	0.8
GRAPEFRUIT, RAW, PINK&RED&WHITE, ALL AREAS		8.08	1.1	0.6
GRAPEFRUIT, RAW, PINK&RED, ALL AREAS		7.68	0.0	0.6
GRAPEFRUIT, RAW, PINK&RED, CALIFORNIA&ARIZONA		9.69	0.0	0.5
GRAPEFRUIT, RAW, PINK&RED, FLORIDA		7.5	1.1	0.6
GRAPEFRUIT, RAW, WHITE, ALL AREAS		8.41	1.1	0.7
GRAPEFRUIT, RAW, WHITE, CALIFORNIA		9.09	0.0	0.9
GRAPEFRUIT, RAW, WHITE, FLORIDA		8.19	0.0	0.6
GRAPEFRUIT JUC, CND, UNSWTND		8.96	0.1	0.5

Food Description	Nutrient	Limit 50 gm/D Carbohydrate/wt gm/100 gm	20-30 gm/D Fiber/wt gm/100 gm	45-63 gm/D Protein/wt gm/100 gm
GRAPEFRUIT JUC, WHITE, RAW		9.2	0.1	0.5
GRAPES, AMERICAN TYPE (SLIP SKN), RAW		17.15	1.0	0.6
GRAPES, RED OR GRN(EURO TYPE VAR, IE; THOMPSON SDLESS), RAW		17.77	1.0	0.7
GUAVAS, COMMON, RAW		11.88	5.4	0.8
GUAVAS, STRAWBY, RAW		17.36	5.4	0.6
GUAVA SAUCE, COOKED		9.48	3.6	0.3
KIWI FRUIT, (CHINESE GOOSEBIES), FRSH, RAW		14.88	3.4	1.0
KUMQUATS, RAW		16.43	6.6	0.9
LEMONS, RAW, WITHOUT PEEL		9.32	2.8	1.1
LEMONS, RAW, WITH PEEL		10.7	4.7	1.2
LEMON JUICE, RAW		8.63	0.4	0.4
LIMES, RAW		10.54	2.8	0.7
LIME JUICE, RAW		9.01	0.4	0.4
LIME JUC, CND OR BTLD, UNSWTND		6.69	0.4	0.3
LOGANBIES, FROZEN		13.02	4.9	1.5
MANGOS, RAW		17	1.8	0.5
MELONS, CANTALOUPE, RAW		8.36	0.8	0.9
MELONS, CASABA, RAW		6.2	0.8	0.9
MELONS, HONEYDEW, RAW		9.18	0.6	0.5
MELON BALLS, FROZEN		7.94	0.7	0.8
NECTARINES, RAW		11.78	1.6	0.9
OLIVES, RIPE, CND (SMALL-EXTRA LRG)		6.26	3.2	0.8
OLIVES, RIPE, CND (JUMBO-SUPER COLOSSAL)		5.61	2.5	1.0
ORANGES, RAW, ALL COMM VAR		11.75	2.4	0.9
ORANGES, RAW, CALIFORNIA, VALENCIAS		11.89	2.5	1.0
ORANGES, RAW, CALIFORNIA, NAVELS		11.63	2.4	1.0
ORANGES, RAW, FLORIDA		11.54	2.4	0.7
ORANGE JUICE, RAW		10.4	0.2	0.7
TANGERINES, (MANDARIN ORANGES), RAW		11.19	2.3	0.6
TANGERINE JUICE, RAW		10.1	0.2	0.5
PAPAYAS, RAW		9.81	1.8	0.6
PAPAYA NECTAR, CANNED		14.51	0.6	0.2
PEACHES, RAW		11.1	2.0	0.7
PEARS, RAW		15.11	2.4	0.4
PERSIMMONS, JAPANESE, RAW		18.59	3.6	0.6
PERSIMMONS, NATIVE, RAW		33.5	0.0	0.8
PINEAPPLE, RAW		12.39	1.2	0.4
PINEAPPLE JUC, CND, UNSWTND, WO/ VIT C		13.78	0.2	0.3
PLUMS, RAW		13.01	1.5	0.8
POMEGRANATES, RAW		17.17	0.6	1.0
PRICKLY PEARS, RAW		9.57	3.6	0.7
QUINCES, RAW		15.3	1.9	0.4
RASPBIES, RAW		11.57	6.8	0.9
RHUBARB, RAW		4.54	1.8	0.9
RHUBARB, FROZEN, UNCOOKED		5.1	1.8	0.6
STRAWBIES, RAW		7.02	2.3	0.6

Food Description	Nutrient	Limit 50 gm/D Carbohydrate/wt gm/100 gm	20-30 gm/D Fiber/wt gm/100 gm	45-63 gm/D Protein/wt gm/100 gm
STRAWBIES, FRZ, UNSWTND		9.13	2.1	0.4
WATERMELON, RAW		7.18	0.5	0.6
PEARS, ASIAN, RAW		10.65	3.6	0.5
ALFALFA SEEDS, SPROUTED, RAW		3.78	2.5	4.0
ARTICHOKES, (GLOBE OR FRENCH), CKD, BLD, DRND, WO/SALT		11.18	5.4	3.5
ARTICHOKES, (GLOBE OR FRENCH), FRZ, CKD, BLD, DRND, WO/SALT		9.18	4.6	3.1
ASPARAGUS, RAW		4.54	2.1	2.3
ASPARAGUS, CKD, BLD, DRND		4.23	1.6	2.6
ASPARAGUS, FRZ, CKD, BLD, DRND, WO/SALT		4.87	1.6	3.0
BAMBOO SHOOTS, CKD, BLD, DRND, WO/SALT		1.92	1.0	1.5
BEANS, BLACK, MATURE SEEDS, CKD, BLD, WO/SALT		23.71	8.7	8.9
BEANS, BLACK TURTLE SOUP, MATURE SEEDS, CKD, BLD, WO/SALT		24.35	5.3	8.2
BEANS, BLACK TURTLE SOUP, MATURE SEEDS, CND		16.56	6.9	6.0
BEANS, CRANBY (ROMAN), MATURE SEEDS, CKD, BLD, WO/SALT		24.46	10.0	9.3
BEANS, CRANBY (ROMAN), MATURE SEEDS, CND		15.12	6.3	5.5
BEANS, FRENCH, MATURE SEEDS, CKD, BLD, WO/SALT		24.02	9.4	7.1
BEANS, GREAT NORTHERN, MATURE SEEDS, CKD, BLD, WO/SALT		21.09	7.0	8.3
BEANS, GREAT NORTHERN, MATURE SEEDS, CND		21.03	4.9	7.4
BEANS, KIDNEY, ALL TYPES, MATURE SEEDS, CKD, BLD, WO/SALT		22.81	6.4	8.7
BEANS, KIDNEY, ALL TYPES, MATURE SEEDS, CND		14.88	3.5	5.2
BEANS, NAVY, MATURE SEEDS, CKD, BLD, WO/SALT		26.31	6.4	8.7
BEANS, NAVY, MATURE SEEDS, CND		20.45	5.1	7.5
BEANS, PINK, MATURE SEEDS, CKD, BLD, WO/SALT		27.91	5.3	9.1
BEANS, PINTO, MATURE SEEDS, CKD, BLD, WO/SALT		25.65	8.6	8.2
BEANS, PINTO, MATURE SEEDS, CND		15.25	4.6	4.9
BEANS, SML WHITE, MATURE SEEDS, CKD, BLD, WO/SALT		25.81	10.4	9.0
BEANS, YEL, MATURE SEEDS, CKD, BLD, WO/SALT		25.27	10.4	9.2
BROADBEANS (FAVA BNS), MATURE SEEDS, CKD, BLD, WO/SALT		19.65	5.4	7.6
LENTILS, MATURE SEEDS, CKD, BLD, WO/SALT		20.14	7.9	9.0
MUNG BNS, MATURE SEEDS, CKD, BLD, WO/SALT		19.14	7.6	7.0
MUNG BNS, MATURE SEEDS, SPROUTED, RAW		5.93	1.8	3.0
PEAS, SPLIT, MATURE SEEDS, CKD, BLD, WO/SALT		21.11	8.3	8.3
REFRIED BEANS, CANNED (INCL USDA COMMODITY)		15.53	5.3	5.5
SOYBEANS, MATURE SEEDS, RSTD, SALTED		33.56	17.7	35.2
SOYBEANS, MATURE SEEDS, DRY RSTD		32.72	8.1	39.6
LIMA BNS, IMMAT SEEDS, CKD, BLD, DRND, WO/SALT		23.64	5.3	6.8
LIMA BNS, IMMAT SEEDS, FRZ, FORDHOOK, CKD, BLD, DRND, WO/SALT		18.8	5.8	6.1
LIMA BNS, IMMAT SEEDS, FRZ, BABY, CKD, BLD, DRND, WO/SALT		19.45	6.0	6.7
BEANS, SNAP, GRN, CKD, BLD, DRND, WO/SALT		7.89	3.2	1.9
BEANS, SNAP, GRN, FRZ, CKD, BLD, DRND WO/SALT		6.45	3.0	1.5
BEETS, RAW		9.56	2.8	1.6
BEETS, CKD, BLD, DRND		9.96	2.0	1.7
BROCCOLI, RAW		5.24	3.0	3.0
BROCCOLI, CKD, BLD, DRND, WO/SALT		5.06	2.9	3.0
BROCCOLI, FRZ, CHOPD OR SPEARS, CKD, BLD, DRND, WO/SALT		5.35	3.0	3.1
BRUSSELS SPROUTS, RAW		8.96	3.8	3.4

Food Description	Nutrient	Limit 50 gm/D Carbohydrate/wt gm/100 gm	20-30 gm/D Fiber/wt gm/100 gm	45-63 gm/D Protein/wt gm/100 gm
BRUSSELS SPROUTS, CKD, BLD, DRND, WO/SALT		8.67	2.6	2.6
BRUSSELS SPROUTS, FRZ, CKD, BLD, DRND, WO/SALT		8.32	4.1	3.6
CABBAGE, RAW		5.43	2.3	1.4
CABBAGE, CKD, BLD, DRND, WO/SALT		4.46	2.3	1.0
CABBAGE, RED, RAW		6.12	2.0	1.4
CABBAGE, RED, CKD, BLD, DRND, WO/SALT		4.64	2.0	1.1
CABBAGE, SAVOY, RAW		6.1	3.1	2.0
CABBAGE, SAVOY, CKD, BLD, DRND, WO/SALT		5.41	2.8	1.8
CABBAGE, CHINESE (PAK-CHOI), RAW		2.18	1.0	1.5
CABBAGE, CHINESE (PAK-CHOI), CKD, BLD, DRND, WO/SALT		1.78	1.6	1.6
CABBAGE, CHINESE (PE-TSAI), RAW		3.23	3.1	1.2
CABBAGE, CHINESE (PE-TSAI), CKD, BLD, DRND, WO/SALT		2.41	2.7	1.5
CARROTS, RAW		10.14	3.0	1.0
CARROTS, CKD, BLD, DRND, WO/SALT		10.48	3.3	1.1
CARROTS, FRZ, CKD, BLD, DRND, WO/SALT		8.25	3.5	1.2
CAULIFLOWER, RAW		5.2	2.5	2.0
CAULIFLOWER, CKD, BLD, DRND, WO/SALT		4.11	2.7	1.8
CAULIFLOWER, FRZ, CKD, BLD, DRND, WO/SALT		3.75	2.7	1.6
CELERIAC, RAW		9.2	1.8	1.5
CELERIAC, CKD, BLD, DRND, WO/SALT		5.9	1.2	1.0
CELERY, RAW		3.65	1.7	0.8
CELERY, CKD, BLD, DRND, WO/SALT		4.01	1.6	0.8
CHARD, SWISS, RAW		3.74	1.6	1.8
CHARD, SWISS, CKD, BLD, DRND, WO/SALT		4.14	2.1	1.9
CHIVES, RAW		4.35	2.5	3.3
COLESLAW, HOME-PREPARED		12.41	1.5	1.3
COLLARDS, RAW		5.69	3.6	2.5
COLLARDS, CKD, BLD, DRND, WO/SALT		4.9	2.8	2.1
CORN, SWT, YEL, CKD, BLD, DRND, WO/SALT		25.11	2.8	3.3
CORN, SWT, YEL, FRZ, KRNLS CUT OFF COB, BLD, DRND, WO/SALT		19.56	2.4	2.8
CORN, SWT, YEL, FRZ, KRNLS ON COB, CKD, BLD, DRND, WO/SALT		22.33	2.8	3.1
YARDLONG BEAN, RAW		8.35	0.0	2.8
YARDLONG BEAN, CKD, BLD, DRND, WO/SALT		9.18	0.0	2.5
CRESS, GARDEN, RAW		5.5	1.1	2.6
CUCUMBER, WITH PEEL, RAW		2.76	0.8	0.7
CUCUMBER, PEELED, RAW		2.5	0.7	0.6
EGGPLANT, RAW		6.07	2.5	1.0
EGGPLANT, CKD, BLD, DRND, WO/SALT		6.64	2.5	0.8
ENDIVE, RAW		3.35	3.1	1.3
GARLIC, RAW		33.07	2.1	6.4
GINGER ROOT, RAW		15.09	2.0	1.7
GOURD, WHITE-FLOWERED (CALABASH), RAW		3.39	0.0	0.6
GOURD, WHITE-FLOWERED (CALABASH), CKD, BLD, DRND, WO/SALT		3.69	0.0	0.6
JERUSALEM-ARTICHOKES, RAW		17.44	1.6	2.0
KALE, RAW		10.01	2.0	3.3
KALE, CKD, BLD, DRND, WO/SALT		5.63	2.0	1.9

Food Description	Nutrient	Limit 50 gm/D Carbohydrate/wt gm/100 gm	20-30 gm/D Fiber/wt gm/100 gm	45-63 gm/D Protein/wt gm/100 gm
KALE, FRZ, CKD, BLD, DRND, WO/SALT		5.24	2.0	2.8
KOHLRABI, RAW		6.2	3.6	1.7
KOHLRABI, CKD, BLD, DRND, WO/SALT		6.69	1.1	1.8
LAMBSQUARTERS, RAW		7.3	4.0	4.2
LAMBSQUARTERS, CKD, BLD, DRND, WO/SALT		5	2.1	3.2
LEEKS, (BULB&LOWER LEAF-PORTION), RAW		14.15	1.8	1.5
LEEKS, (BULB&LOWER LEAF-PORTION), CKD, BLD, DRND, WO/SALT		7.62	1.0	0.8
LENTILS, SPROUTED, RAW		22.14	0.0	9.0
LENTILS, SPROUTED, CKD, STIR-FRIED, WO/SALT		21.25	0.0	8.8
LETTUCE, BUTTERHEAD (INCL BOSTON&BIBB TYPES), RAW		2.32	1.0	1.3
LETTUCE, COS OR ROMAINE, RAW		2.37	1.7	1.6
LETTUCE, ICEBERG (INCL CRISPHEAD TYPES), RAW		2.09	1.4	1.0
LETTUCE, LOOSELEAF, RAW		3.5	1.9	1.3
MUSHROOMS, RAW		4.08	1.2	2.9
MUSHROOMS, CKD, BLD, DRND, WO/SALT		5.14	2.2	2.2
MUSHROOMS, PORTABELLA, RAW		5.07	1.5	2.5
MUSHROOMS, BROWN, ITALIAN, OR CRIMINI, RAW		4.12	0.6	2.5
MUSHROOMS, SHIITAKE, DRIED		75.37	11.5	9.6
MUSHROOM, OYSTER, RAW		6.22	2.4	4.1
FUNGI, CLOUD EARS, DRIED		73	70.1	9.3
MUSHROOMS, STRAW, CND, DRND SOL		4.65	2.5	3.8
MUSHROOMS, SHIITAKE, CKD, WO/SALT		14.28	2.1	1.6
NEW ZEALAND SPINACH, RAW		2.5	0.0	1.5
NEW ZEALAND SPINACH, CKD, BLD, DRND, WO/SALT		2.2	0.0	1.3
OKRA, RAW		7.63	3.2	2.0
OKRA, CKD, BLD, DRND, WO/SALT		7.21	2.5	1.9
OKRA, FRZ, CKD, BLD, DRND, WO/SALT		5.75	2.8	2.1
ONIONS, RAW		8.63	1.8	1.2
ONIONS, CKD, BLD, DRND, WO/SALT		10.15	1.4	1.4
ONIONS, DEHYDRATED FLAKES		83.28	9.2	9.0
ONIONS, SPRING OR SCALLIONS (INCL TOPS&BULB), RAW		7.34	2.6	1.8
ONIONS, WELSH, RAW		6.5	0.0	1.9
PARSNIPS, RAW		17.99	4.9	1.2
PARSNIPS, CKD, BLD, DRND, WO/SALT		19.53	4.0	1.3
PEAS, EDIBLE-PODDED, RAW		7.56	2.6	2.8
PEAS, EDIBLE-PODDED, CKD, BLD, DRND, WO/SALT		7.05	2.8	3.3
PEAS, EDIBLE-PODDED, FRZ, CKD, BLD, DRND, WO/SALT		9.02	3.1	3.5
PEAS, GREEN, RAW		14.46	5.1	5.4
PEAS, GRN, CKD, BLD, DRND, WO/SALT		15.64	5.5	5.4
PEAS, GRN, FRZ, CKD, BLD, DRND, WO/SALT		14.26	5.5	5.2
PEPPERS, HOT CHILI, GRN, CND, PODS, EXCLUDING SEEDS, SOL&LIQS		5.1	1.3	0.9
PEPPERS, SWEET, GREEN, RAW		6.43	1.8	0.9
PEPPERS, SWT, GRN, CKD, BLD, DRND, WO/SALT		6.7	1.2	0.9
PEPPERS, SWT, GRN, FRZ, CHOPD, BLD, DRND, WO/SALT		3.9	0.9	1.0
POKEBY SHOOTS, (POKE), RAW		3.7	1.7	2.6
POKEBY SHOOTS, (POKE), CKD, BLD, DRND, WO/SALT		3.1	1.5	2.3

Food Description	Nutrient	Limit 50 gm/D Carbohydrate/wt gm/100 gm	20-30 gm/D Fiber/wt gm/100 gm	45-63 gm/D Protein/wt gm/100 gm
POTATOES, RAW, FLESH&SKN		17.98	1.6	2.1
PUMPKIN, RAW		6.5	0.5	1.0
PUMPKIN, CKD, BLD, DRND, WO/SALT		4.89	1.1	0.7
PUMPKIN, CND, WO/SALT		8.08	2.9	1.1
PURSLANE, RAW		3.43	0.0	1.3
PURSLANE, CKD, BLD, DRND, WO/SALT		3.55	0.0	1.5
RADISHES, RAW		3.59	1.6	0.6
RADISHES, ORIENTAL, RAW		4.11	1.6	0.6
RADISHES, ORIENTAL, CKD, BLD, DRND, WO/SALT		3.43	1.6	0.7
RADISHES, ORIENTAL, DRIED		63.37	0.0	7.9
RUTABAGAS, RAW		8.13	2.5	1.2
RUTABAGAS, CKD, BLD, DRND, WO/SALT		8.74	1.8	1.3
SOY PROTEIN ISOLATE		7.36	5.6	80.7
SPINACH, RAW		3.5	2.7	2.9
SPINACH, CKD, BLD, DRND, WO/SALT		3.75	2.4	3.0
SPINACH, FRZ, CHOPD OR LEAF, CKD, BLD, DRND, WO/SALT		5.34	3.0	3.1
SQUASH, SMMR, CROOK & STRAIGHTNECK, RAW		4.04	1.9	0.9
SQUASH, SMMR, CROOK & STRAIGHTNECK, CKD, BLD, DRND, WO/SALT		4.31	1.4	0.9
SQUASH, SMMR, CROOK & STRAIGHTNECK, FRZ, CKD, BLD, DRND, WO/SALT		5.54	1.4	1.3
SQUASH, SUMMER, SCALLOP, RAW		3.84	0.0	1.2
SQUASH, SMMR, SCALLOP, CKD, BLD, DRND, WO/SALT		3.3	1.9	1.0
SQUASH, SMMR, ZUCCHINI, INCL SKN, RAW		2.9	1.2	1.2
SQUASH, SMMR, ZUCCHINI, INCL SKN, CKD, BLD, DRND, WO/SALT		3.93	1.4	0.6
SQUASH, SMMR, ZUCCHINI, INCL SKN, FRZ, CKD, BLD, DRND, WO/SALT		3.56	1.3	1.2
SQUASH, WINTER, ACORN, RAW		10.42	1.5	0.8
SQUASH, WNTR, ACORN, CKD, BKD, WO/SALT		14.58	4.4	1.1
SQUASH, WNTR, ACORN, CKD, BLD, MSHD, WO/SALT		8.78	2.6	0.7
SQUASH, WNTR, BUTTERNUT, RAW		11.69	0.0	1.0
SQUASH, WNTR, BUTTERNUT, CKD, BKD, WO/SALT		10.49	0.0	0.9
SQUASH, WNTR, BUTTERNUT, FRZ, UNPREP		14.41	1.3	1.8
SQUASH, WNTR, BUTTERNUT, FRZ, CKD, BLD, WO/SALT		10.05	0.0	1.2
SQUASH, WINTER, HUBBARD, RAW		8.7	0.0	2.0
SQUASH, WNTR, HUBBARD, CKD, BKD, WO/SALT		10.81	0.0	2.5
SQUASH, WNTR, HUBBARD, CKD, BLD, MSHD, WO/SALT		6.45	2.9	1.5
SQUASH, WNTR, SPAGHETTI, RAW		6.91	0.0	0.6
SQUASH, WNTR, SPAGHETTI, CKD, BLD, DRND, OR BKD, WO/SALT		6.46	1.4	0.7
SWEETPOTATO, RAW		24.28	3.0	1.7
SWEETPOTATO, CKD, BKD IN SKN, WO/SALT		24.27	3.0	1.7
SWEETPOTATO, CKD, BLD, WO/SKN, WO/SALT		24.28	1.8	1.7
TOMATOES, GREEN, RAW		5.1	1.1	1.2
TOMATOES, RED, RIPE, RAW, YEAR RND AVERAGE		4.64	1.1	0.9
TOMATOES, RED, RIPE, CKD, BLD, WO/SALT		5.83	1.0	1.1
TOMATOES, RED, RIPE, CND, WHL, REG PK		4.37	1.0	0.9
TOMATOES, RED, RIPE, CND, STWD		6.78	1.0	1.0
TOMATOES, RED, RIPE, CND, WEDGES IN TOMATO JUC		6.31	0.0	0.8

Food Description	Nutrient	Limit 50 gm/D Carbohydrate/wt gm/100 gm	20-30 gm/D Fiber/wt gm/100 gm	45-63 gm/D Protein/wt gm/100 gm
TOMATOES, RED, RIPE, CND, W/GRN CHILIES		3.62	0.0	0.7
TOMATO JUC, CND, W/SALT		4.23	0.4	0.8
TOMATO PRODUCTS, CND, PASTE, WO/SALT		19.3	4.1	3.7
TOMATO PRODUCTS, CND, PUREE, WO/SALT		9.56	2.0	1.7
TURNIPS, RAW		6.23	1.8	0.9
TURNIPS, CKD, BLD, DRND, WO/SALT		4.9	2.0	0.7
TURNIPS, FRZ, CKD, BLD, DRND, WO/SALT		4.35	2.0	1.5
VINESPINACH, (BASELLA), RAW		3.4	0.0	1.8
WATERCHESTNUTS, CHINESE, (MATAI), RAW		23.94	3.0	1.4
WATERCHESTNUTS, CHINESE, CND, SOL&LIQUIDS		12.43	2.5	0.9
WATERCRESS, RAW		1.29	1.5	2.3
YAM, RAW		27.89	4.1	1.5
YAM, CKD, BLD, DRND, OR BKD, WO/SALT		27.6	3.9	1.5
YAMBEAN (JICAMA), RAW		8.82	4.9	0.7
YAMBEAN (JICAMA), CKD, BLD, DRND, WO/SALT		8.82	0.0	0.7
WASABI, ROOT, RAW		23.54	7.7	4.8
ALMONDS, RAW		19.74	11.8	21.3
ALMONDS, BLANCHED		19.94	10.4	21.9
ALMONDS, DRY RSTD, W & WO/SALT		19.29	11.8	22.1
ALMONDS, OIL RSTD, W & WO/SALT		17.68	10.5	21.2
BRAZILNUTS, DRIED, UNBLANCHED		12.8	5.4	14.3
CASHEW NUTS, DRY RSTD, W & WO/SALT		32.69	3.0	15.3
CASHEW NUTS, OIL RSTD, W & WO/SALT		28.52	3.8	16.2
CHESTNUTS, EUROPEAN, RAW, PEELED		44.17	0.0	1.6
CHESTNUTS, EUROPEAN, RSTD		52.96	5.1	3.2
CHESTNUTS, EUROPEAN, BLD&STMD		27.76	0.0	2.0
COCONUT MEAT, RAW		15.23	9.0	3.3
COCONUT MEAT, DRIED (DESICCATED), NOT SWTND		24.41	16.3	6.9
COCONUT CRM, CND (LIQ EXPRESSED FROM GRATED MEAT)		8.35	2.2	2.7
COCONUT MILK, RAW (LIQ EXPRESSED FROM GRATED MEAT&H2O)		5.54	2.2	2.3
COCONUT MILK, CND (LIQ EXPRESSED FROM GRATED MEAT&H2O)		2.81	0.0	2.0
COCONUT H2O (LIQ FROM COCONUTS)		3.71	1.1	0.7
HAZELNUTS OR FILBERTS		16.7	9.7	15.0
MACADAMIA NUTS, RAW		13.82	8.6	7.9
MACADAMIA NUTS, DRY RSTD, WO/SALT		13.38	8.0	7.8
MACADAMIA NUTS, DRY RSTD, W/SALT		12.83	8.0	7.8
MIXED NUTS, DRY RSTD, W/PNUTS, W & WO/SALT		25.35	9.0	17.3
MIXED NUTS, OIL RSTD, W/PNUTS, W & WO/SALT		21.41	9.9	16.8
MIXED NUTS, OIL RSTD, WO/PNUTS, W & WO/SALT		22.27	5.5	15.5
PEANUTS, ALL TYPES, RAW		16.14	8.5	25.8
PEANUTS, ALL TYPES, CKD, BLD, W/SALT		21.26	8.8	13.5
PEANUTS, ALL TYPES, OIL-ROASTED, W/SALT		18.93	9.2	26.4
PEANUTS, ALL TYPES, DRY-ROASTED, W/SALT		21.51	8.0	23.7
PECANS		13.86	9.6	9.2
PECANS, DRY RSTD, W & WO/SALT		13.5	9.5	9.5
PECANS, OIL RSTD, W & WO/SALT		13.01	9.5	9.2

Food Description	Nutrient	Limit 50 gm/D Carbohydrate/wt gm/100 gm	20-30 gm/D Fiber/wt gm/100 gm	45-63 gm/D Protein/wt gm/100 gm
PINE NUTS, PIGNOLIA, DRIED		14.22	4.5	24.0
PISTACHIO NUTS, RAW		29.19	10.0	20.5
PISTACHIO NUTS, DRY RSTD, WO/SALT		27.99	10.3	21.2
PISTACHIO NUTS, DRY RSTD, W/SALT		27.13	10.3	21.2
PUMPKIN&SQUASH SD KRNLS, RSTD, W/SALT		13.43	3.9	33.0
SESAME SEEDS, WHOLE, DRIED		23.45	11.8	17.7
SESAME SEEDS, WHL, RSTD&TSTD		25.74	14.0	17.0
SUNFLOWER SD KRNLS, OIL RSTD, WO/SALT		14.73	6.8	21.4
WALNUTS, BLACK, DRIED		12.1	5.0	24.4
WALNUTS, ENGLISH		13.71	6.7	15.2
ALCOHOLIC BEV, BEER, REG		3.7	0.2	0.3
ALCOHOLIC BEV, BEER, LT		1.3	0.0	0.2
ALCOHOLIC BEV, DAIQUIRI, PREPARED-FROM-RECIPE		6.8	0.0	0.1
ALCOHOLIC BEV, PINA COLADA, PREPARED-FROM-RECIPE		28.3	0.6	0.4
ALCOHOLIC BEV, TEQUILA SUNRISE, CND		11.3	0.0	0.3
ALCOHOLIC BEV, WHISKEY SOUR, PREP W/H2O, WHISKEY&PDR MIX		15.9	0.0	0.1
ALCOHOLIC BEV, WHISKEY SOUR, CND		13.4	0.1	0.0
WHISKEY SOUR MIX, BTLD, WO/ K&NA		21.4	0.0	0.1
ALCOHOLIC BEV, LIQUEUR, COFFEE, 53 PROOF		46.8	0.0	0.1
ALCOHOLIC BEV, LIQUEUR, COFFEE W/CRM, 34 PROOF		20.9	0.0	2.8
ALCOHOLIC BEV, LIQUEUR, COFFEE, 63 PROOF		32.2	0.0	0.1
ALCOHOLIC BEV, CREME DE MENTHE, 72 PROOF		41.6	0.0	0.0
ALCOHOLIC BEV, DISTILLED, ALL (GIN, RUM, VODKA, WHISKEY) 80 PROOF		0	0.0	0.0
ALCOHOLIC BEV, DISTILLED, GIN, 90 PROOF		0	0.0	0.0
ALCOHOLIC BEV, DISTILLED, RUM, 80 PROOF		0	0.0	0.0
ALCOHOLIC BEV, DISTILLED, VODKA, 80 PROOF		0	0.0	0.0
ALCOHOLIC BEV, DISTILLED, WHISKEY, 86 PROOF		0.1	0.0	0.0
ALCOHOLIC BEV, WINE, DSSRT, SWT		11.8	0.0	0.2
ALCOHOLIC BEV, WINE, DSSRT, DRY		4.1	0.0	0.2
ALCOHOLIC BEV, WINE, TABLE, ALL		1.4	0.0	0.2
ALCOHOLIC BEV, WINE, TABLE, RED		1.7	0.0	0.2
ALCOHOLIC BEV, WINE, TABLE, ROSE		1.4	0.0	0.2
ALCOHOLIC BEV, WINE, TABLE, WHITE		0.8	0.0	0.1
CARBONATED BEV, CLUB SODA		0	0.0	0.0
CARBONATED BEV, CRM SODA		13.3	0.0	0.0
CARBONATED BEV, GINGER ALE		8.7	0.0	0.0
CARBONATED BEV, GRAPE SODA		11.2	0.0	0.0
CARBONATED BEV, LEMON-LIME SODA		10.4	0.0	0.0
CARBONATED BEV, ORANGE		12.3	0.0	0.0
CARBONATED BEV, PEPPER-TYPE, CONTAINS CAFFEINE		10.4	0.0	0.0
CARBONATED BEV, TONIC H2O		8.8	0.0	0.0
CARBONATED BEV, ROOT BEER		10.6	0.0	0.0
COFFEE, BREWED, PREP W/TAP H2O, REGULAR & DECAFFEINATED		0.4	0.0	0.1
COFFEE, BREWED, ESPRESSO, REST-PREP		1.53	0.0	0.0
COFFEE, INST, REG & DECAFFEINATED, PDR, PREP W/H2O		0.4	0.0	0.1
TEA, BREWED, PREP W/TAP H2O, REGULAR & DECAFFEINATED		0.3	0.0	0.0

For more information about this book, please visit:
www.unlimitedpublishing.com/authors
or
www.lowcarbforlife.net

Richard Frankville, D.C.
is also the resident chef at:
www.collectiblemeals.com
"Serve a slice of history at your next dinner party!"

You can receive new recipes by e-mail, free of charge.
Simply send a message to Dr. Frankville:
doc@lowcarbforlife.net
and ask to join his mailing list.

Feedback from readers is always welcome!

Printed in the United States
17389LVS00003BB/67-510